WESTONBIRT

Association News

1930 – 2020

90 years of Westonbirt Association

~ Bono malum superate ~

Westonbirt Association News 2020

Published in paperback and ebook by Hawkesbury Press 2020
Hawkesbury Upton, Gloucestershire, UK GL9 1AS
www.hawkesburypress.com

For further information about the Westonbirt Association,
please contact
Westonbirt School
Tetbury, Gloucestershire, UK, GL8 8QG
www.westonbirt.org

Trunk clipart: **http://clipart-library.com/clipart/55402**
Licence: Not for commercial use

ISBN 978-1-911223-63-4

Also available as an e-book

British Library Cataloguing in Publication Data
A CiP catalogue record for this book is available from the British Library

Contents

Westonbirt Association Officers 2020

EXECUTIVE COMMITTEE

President & Honorary Secretary Mrs Leigh Ralphs
Honorary Treasurer Mrs Karen Broomhead
News Finances and Distribution Mrs Jenny Webb
News Editor Mrs Bridget Bomford
Headmistress Mrs Natasha Dangerfield
Staff Representative Mrs Joy Bell

Co-opted Members
Mrs Serena Jones
Ms Karen Olsen
Mrs Mary Phillips
Mrs Debbie Young

Support Roles
Membership Assistant Mrs Jane Reid
Head of Public Relations & Events Mrs Rhiannon Roche

GENERAL COMMITTEE

The Executive Committee and all the Section Representatives

2020 ANNUAL GENERAL MEETING

Saturday 22nd May 2021

VICE PRESIDENTS
Mrs P Faust
Dr A Grocock
Mrs M Henderson
Mrs G Hylson-Smith
Ms Karen Olsen

HONORARY MEMBERS

Mr R Baggs
Mrs B Bomford
Miss V Byrom-Taylor
Miss D Challis
Mrs S Cole
Miss B D Cooper
Miss N O Davies
Mr P Dixon
Mrs Ann Dunn
Mrs D Elsdon
Mrs S English
Mrs L J Evans
Miss M Evett
Mrs M R Farley
Mrs J Hutchings
Mrs V A Innes
Mrs R J Kingston
Miss J Marr
Miss E M Miller
Miss P E Morris
Mrs H Nickols
Mrs H Owen
Mrs J Paginton
Miss O T Pasco
Mr D Philbey
Mrs M Phillips
Mrs A Potter
Mrs H R Price
Mrs A M Reed
Mrs J Reid
Mrs A Rodber
Mrs D Thombs
Mrs C Tilley
Miss S Urquhart
Mrs M Walding
Miss K S Yates
Mrs D Young

Editorial

Where do I start with this piece in the current circumstances? It's mid-May as I write, and the government has just updated its guidance on relaxing restrictions, and we are being asked to 'stay alert' and to minimise travel and continue social distancing (yet another new phrase for the future!).

Having read through everyone's news, I am very conscious that many, many Association members, from the youngest to the oldest, have had to forego travel plans, gap year aspirations, family reunions, weddings, and many other celebrations. For a few, it may mean that some of these plans never come to fruition, whilst for others the change may lead to something completely unexpected and wonderful; whatever it may be, the Westonbirt spirit will help us all through.

As you are all aware, it hasn't been possible to celebrate ninety years of the Westonbirt Association this year in the ways we'd hoped. The committee had many plans for how to use the wonderful memories and photos sent in by our members as part of the celebrations on 16th May, so when these had to be cancelled we felt we needed a simple way to mark the anniversary within the Association News itself. So just before the Section News, you will find special feature by Angela Potter (Section 27) inspired by the school trunk!

It was lovely to receive the iris e-card, painted so beautifully by Mary Phillips, the kind messages from Natasha and Rhiannon, and, of course, all the material put together with some of the current pupils (yes, girls AND boys!) It really made the day feel special, and we've still got next year's celebrations to look forward to as well!

Like many people interested in the history of the school, I have been reflecting on its past, and comparing the current crisis to the war years at Bowood and Corsham Court. Whilst many of the problems and difficulties are the same, the most significant difference is that during the war years everyone could physically remain together, could support each other practically, and could hug each other when things got rough. I think of the fruit and hop picking camps of those wartime summer holidays, of archive photos showing girls in overalls, arm in arm under the fruit trees, of a letter from the school to parents, telling them what their daughters should take with them to camp, including a ground sheet, if I remember rightly!

We do, of course, have technology and social media now, playing a huge and positive part in helping us keep in touch with family and friends, and providing a means of delivering online lessons, and entertainment, of course! It's life like we've never known it before, with many emotional and financial challenges for us all, to varying degrees.

But we've proved that it is possible to live without rushing here, there, and everywhere, that we can get through without all the travelling we'd planned to do, without having to go out and buy things all the time; things are out of stock, so we make do, and find it's not so difficult after all…

It's as if the planet, with its non-human inhabitants, which we have for so long taken for granted, abused and exploited, is gifting us all with a time of reflection, a time to stand back and assess what's really important, to give us the chance of making the 'new normal' caring and sustainable…

At the end of the day, it's the same for us as it was for our Westonbirt predecessors in the 1940's; we all have the chance to make the world a better place, to use adversity as the starting point for positive change. Westonbirt is good at positive change, it's good at being there for people, good at innovation (in 1928 it was, after all, described by the press as 'a freak school with no rules'!), good at caring, good at helping its students be the best they can be, and good at helping people fulfil their dreams and ambitions. Probably some of these dreams and ambitions will change as a result of COVID-19, but, whatever they may be, the Westonbirt spirit will be there for us all, underpinning all our endeavours, and helping us shape a better future.

Very best wishes to everyone for good health, happiness, and success with those endeavours!

Bridget Bomford

President's Report

As I write this report, we have entered the fourth week of lockdown in the UK. Who would have thought that the Association's 90th Anniversary celebrations would be cancelled because of a pandemic? It feels very surreal. We had been expecting a record number of alumni to return to Westonbirt and enjoy the special birthday lunch on 16th May, but it has now been postponed until May 2021. Hopefully by then COVID-19 will be behind us, and we will still be able to enjoy our 90th, even if it's a little later than expected on Saturday 22nd May 2021.

My thanks once again to Rhiannon Roche for her help with organising the celebrations and assisting the Association. Rhiannon has moved from being PA to the Head to a new role as Head of Public Relations and Events, and we are delighted that she will continue with her responsibility for Alumni Relations. However, for the moment, Rhiannon has been furloughed and may not be able to answer emails until the School goes back. The best way to get in touch in the meantime is to email database@westonbirt.gloucs.sch.uk.

Sadly, we were also unable to hold the annual Leavers' Tea in April as the pupils had already left! Westonbirt, like all other schools, has had to close temporarily during this outbreak, which meant that they bid farewell to Year 13 at the end of the spring term. I would like to thank Mary Phillips for introducing them to the Association on our behalf at their Leavers' Assembly and presenting them with their amaryllis charms. We welcome Eloise, who was our Study One Rep, as the new Representative for Section 89.

We had also been planning to hold an inaugural Association v School golf match in May on the Westonbirt Golf Course. This again will have to go on hold and hopefully be moved to later this year or into next. If anyone would be interested in playing, please email Rhiannon Roche, Head of Public Relations and Events, at rhiannon.roche@westonbirtschool.uk.

The Celia Graham Lacrosse Tournament for Alumni v School is due to be played on Saturday 12 September 2020, subject to COVID-19. If you would like further details, or to sign up, please email Rhiannon Roche at rhiannon.roche@westonbirtschool.uk.

When life goes back to normal, please remember Westonbirt's Skill for Life programme, run by Mrs Jo Edwards, which includes personal, social and health education and broadens minds and opportunities for pupils. Any alumni who would like to take part in the future by delivering sessions to years 7-13 about their own experiences should email Rhiannon Roche at rhiannon.roche@westonbirtschool.uk.

Alumni can get involved in other ways too, as did our own Debbie Young, published author and recently retired Editor of the Association's News, who returned to Westonbirt for World Book Day. The Head of English, Tabatha Sheehan, was delighted, and says 'It was wonderful to see Debbie interacting and sharing her writing with so many of our pupils.' For further information on Debbie's books, visit her website, www.authordebbieyoung.com. Her latest novel is set in a girl's boarding school!

The Association continues to support the Memorial Bursary, a fund set up in the late 1940s in memory of the five former Westonbirt pupils who lost their lives during the Second World War whilst members of the armed forces, civil defence, or nursing services. Each year the Memorial Bursary is used to help fund the sixth form fees of one or more pupils who would otherwise not be able to stay on at Westonbirt. I personally find it a real privilege to be able to support outstanding students in this way, and I would encourage anyone who is thinking of donating to the Memorial Bursary fund, or considering bequeathing a sum of money, not to hesitate, as you could be helping to change or shape a young person's life. Further information about this can be found at the back of this News Magazine.

Upon special request, the Association has agreed to sponsor Isobel, a Year 12 girl, through the Leith's Certificate in Food and Wine, which is run as a co-curricular activity in the sixth form. The course concentrates on excellent skills of food preparation and presentation, and the students prepare two or three dishes every week for five terms.

My thanks as always go to all the Section Reps who have gathered together the News from their Sections in spite of the challenges of COVID-19, to Bridget Bomford, our Editor, for editing and producing it, to Serena Jones, Karen Olsen and Karen Broomhead for proof-reading, and to Jenny Webb distributing the hard copies. It is always such an interesting read and this year is ideal for browsing through during the lockdown!

Bridget has been collecting memories from alumni in order to produce something for our 90th, originally planned for the celebrations in May this year. As these have now been re-scheduled for next year, you can continue to send memories in to her if you wish at b.bomford@hotmail.co.uk.

On behalf of the Association, I would like to wish you all good health and confirm our continued support for Westonbirt during these unprecedented times. I hope that many of you will use this time as an opportunity to reconnect and get back in touch with one another.

Leigh Ralphs

Headmistress's Report

As I write this, during the Association's 90th year, Westonbirt is in the process of fulfilling education in an online environment. Five weeks into lockdown, I cannot think the site has ever been so quiet. Over this period, we have gained new 'pupils' - as ours are all safely stowed with their families, the roe deer, foxes and rabbits claim the grounds, and the birds make the most of their myriad of nesting spaces, perching to preen feathers and deliver some fantastic music for us. One could say therefore, we are as busy as usual, but without the students, we are not the same.

I can only imagine that the last time the school saw such disruption was in the Bowood years, as staff and students were sent on to different locations, continuing their education in remote, different, and makeshift environments. Were stakes as high? I suspect they were, and as a silent enemy makes its way around the world, perhaps times are not so altered.

Usually at this time the school would have been mid-preparation for our annual and very successful Picnic in the Park and looking forward to a celebratory 90th anniversary lunch with the Association ahead of the concert. We had been delighted with the enthusiastic response to this event and were very much looking forward to welcoming a large number of alumni, spanning several generations and continents, to Westonbirt on 16th May. For the first time, we would have been presenting the Year 7 boys in concert; our exciting strategic step forward as a school and one which has proved very successful. Despite challenging times, we are set to see these Year 7 pupils working through to Year 8 and adding a new year group in Year 9. With a 50:50 Year 7 intake, we are pleased that this development will result in one of the largest school rolls in ten years! I am sorry we cannot see those of you who were hoping to join us in May, but we already have an alternative date in the calendar for next year – Saturday 22nd May.

Following some significant donations to HoWT, the lake, which has been empty following a fallen tree splitting the bed in 2013, is being fixed, and an expert crew is filling cracks and pulling overgrown undergrowth back to find the original edges, revealing a shape many of you will remember. Also unearthed has been a signature cut into the bed of the lake which we believe confirms the original feature was completed in 1875.

I hope that the focus on the new coeducational cohort, plus this renovation of one of the original features of the House, will indicate to you that Westonbirt continues to move progressively forward, yet retains the sense of heritage and propriety which will ensure that we remain in touch with our traditional values in a modern educational setting.

Wishing you all good health.

Mrs Natasha Dangerfield

Careers Events Supported by Association Members

One of the main ways in which association members contribute to the school each year is through their involvement with the Careers Events Programme, run by Mrs Jo Edwards, but unfortunately, these events have been another casualty of COVID-19 this year.

Of course, alumni can, and do, support the school in other ways too. This year, in early March, just before the lockdown began, our former Association News Editor, novelist, and publishing guru, Debbie Young, spent a week in school, which included World Book Day, working with students, and sharing with them her knowledge on all aspects of being a writer. Head of English Tabitha Sheenan, sent the following report:

The English Department are really keen to show our gratitude to Debbie Young - she spent a week with us for World Book Day (we even made it World Book Week!) and it was wonderful to see Debbie interacting and sharing her writing with so many of our pupils. Debbie kindly came into all of our KS3 lessons and spoke about what it takes to be a writer and the skills she had learnt through self-publishing and shared her tips in becoming better readers and writers. The pupils were delighted to meet her and see her work; particularly how it had been so inspired by her time at Westonbirt!

Beyond these lessons, Debbie also judged our Inter-House Reading competition - she was so impressed by the ambitious extracts chosen and the confidence of our readers and gave a wonderful speech about the importance of literature.

We were then due to have Debbie in for a lecture on the Friday evening - unfortunately, this had to be postponed, but we look forward to when we can reschedule it!

Many thanks, Debbie, for your time, efforts, and love of literature.

If anyone else out there has skills and expertise that could be shared with the school, please do get in contact with Rhiannon Roche at rhiannon.roche@westonbirtschool.uk. She will be pleased to put you in touch with the relevant school department.

Deaths Notified Since 2019

Name	Section	Date of death
Sheila Fraser	8	17 February 2019
Maureen Burnell (Melvin)	18	8 October 2018
Robin Jane Wells	19	29 June 2019
Angela Noel Bates	21	17 October 2019
Helen Louise Hyder (Gordon-Smith)	21	5 December 2015
Pauline Hathorn (Horrocks)	26	Late 2019
Angela Knapp (Boswell)	(27 cohort)	NK (Left 1957)
Ann Thelma Williamson	27	29 May 2020
Clare Carr-Archer (Henton)	30	15 August 2019
Carolyn Reynolds (Mathison)	30	May 2019
(Margaret) Patricia Miller (Isaac)	(30 cohort)	12 August 2017
(Eirene) Miranda Harris (Dodd)	41	28 October 2019
Jane Wroebel (Wakefield)	41	
Joanna Cobb	49	20 September 2019
Cynthia Kathleen Bryan (Ashley Cooper, then Duncan)	6	31 December 2017

The School Trunk

I have a fond memory of my school trunk. Not the trunk itself, but the pleasure of opening it. It would be very neatly packed, with a fitted tray for lighter things at the top and had the marvellous smell of new clothes and shoes. A new term. A new start.

The trunks didn't accompany us on our journey to school though, especially as most of us came by train. They went either by PLA (Passenger Luggage in Advance) or a haulage firm that would collect and deliver door to door (Carter Patterson or Pickford's). They would precede us, and the school workmen would have to carry them upstairs to await our arrival (there was no lift then).All the items on the lengthy 'clothes 'list had to be named before going into the trunk. This list included sheets and pillowcases, a travel rug, two table napkins, a dirty clothes bag, shoe bags and twenty-four handkerchiefs. The woven Cash's tapes, embroidered with my name and house number, had been ordered, and these were sewn into every item on the list.

There was underwear to go into the trunk as well. We had to have grey bloomers (for gym), vests, lisle stockings and suspender belts, socks for games, and short white ones for the summer. If it wasn't listed, my mother didn't provide it. I had only been at school for a few days, when I realised that I should have brought 'white cotton linings' (underpants to you and me).

Additional 'regulation' items had to go in the trunk as well; these included a maroon cardigan, white poplin shirts and white aertex shirts, a maroon tie, a long-sleeved white sweater (for games) and specific shoes. As far as I recall we had lace-ups, 'house shoes', and (in the summer) sandals, all of which had to conform to strict descriptions but could be bought locally.

Miss Ayres (affectionately known as Auntie) ran the second-hand cupboard in Badminton House, which helped fill many a trunk in the austere post-war years. The cloak, the grey tweed skirt, the v. necked grey jumper with maroon stripes round the neck, the pleated shorts, the grey flannel suit, the pink silk dress (called the pink sack), and the maroon felt hat, could all be purchased there.

Girls' trunks contained many identical garments, but in one thing there was choice - the dress we wore for the evening. There were strict guidelines, but also a degree of variation, particularly in colour. Following a post-lunch 'rest' in the dormitory we had games after which we could change into our dresses for tea, (without having a shower: there were none, and baths were rationed to one evening a week).

Each morning, before breakfast, having dressed in the clothes transported in our trusty trunks, we had 'inspection'. In winter months, unless you had gym, you had to wear the grey skirt, the white poplin shirt, with maroon tie, the v. necked jumper and the beige lisle stockings. Jewellery was not allowed at all, with the exception of a plain tie pin, regimental badge, or crucifix on a neck chain.

My trunk made mostly of plywood, and well battered from many train journeys, sadly fell apart soon after I left school, but I still have some of my hankies, and one of the table napkins with the school laundry mark! I even have the clothes bag and shoe bags - they were, and still are hideous! The memory of the smell of that packed trunk is still with me though!

Angela Potter (Section 27)

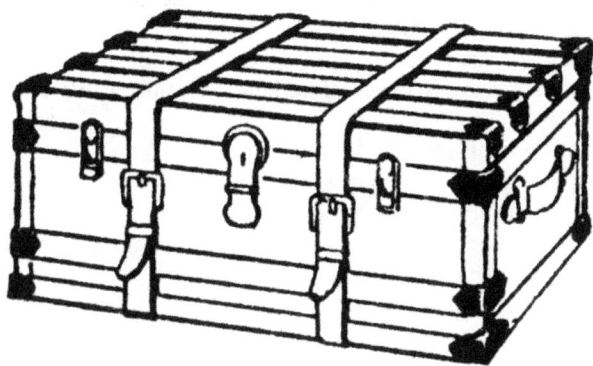

SECTION NEWS

Thank You to Section Representatives

The Association is enormously grateful for the hard work and attention to detail shown each year by the Section Representatives, who volunteer to collect and collate the news from their former classmates. Modern technology makes this much easier than years ago, with many of even the most senior members sending in their news by email. Some members have also found social media, particularly Facebook and Twitter, useful for newsgathering.

Thank You to Section Members

We are always pleased to hear members' news, so if you're a regular respondent, thank you very much for continuing to keep us posted.

If you've not sent in your own news for a while, please don't hold back. Even if you feel you have nothing to report, we still like to know that you are alive and well, and that we have the right contact details for you. We also love hearing reminiscences about your own time at Westonbirt.

Youngest Sections First

We're continuing the practice of starting with news from the most recent leavers. In the early, heady days of higher education and careers, keeping communication channels open with their *alma mater* may not be a top priority, so with the newest sections at the front they won't have too far to look to catch up on their Section's news, and we do appreciate even the briefest of reports!

In all sections, we have listed members in alphabetical order by their current surname, to make it easier to find your friends.

If reading any of their news makes you hanker after a nostalgic trip back to Westonbirt, we'd love to see you at our annual Association Day, and the school also welcomes visits by appointment all year round.

To Arrange a Visit or for Information

To arrange to visit, or for any information regarding the Association, such as the current contact details for your Section Rep, please do not hesitate to contact Mrs Rhiannon Roche, Head of Public Relations and Events, via her school email address, rroche@westonbirt.gloucs.sch.uk, or by telephoning her on 01666 880333

Staff Section

Section Representative:
Mrs Mary Phillips

Mrs Joy Bell I am still enjoying teaching at Westonbirt and spending much of my holiday time in Brittany, but the greatest news this year is how we have all coped with the COVID-19 pandemic. The school year of 2019/20 is one we will always remember - we ended the spring term a week early, as Boris Johnson closed English schools on 20th March. We moved to remote learning at that point, conducting lessons with our classes using the internet in the final week of term. As I write this, at the end of the Easter holiday, staff are gearing up to continue running lessons remotely. For someone such as myself with limited technical skills and understanding it has indeed been a steep learning curve and has possibly helped me to understand how some of my pupils may feel when I'm trying to explain something that seems so easy to me. But we have made tremendous progress in a short time and are certainly doing our very best to ensure that good quality teaching and learning continues to happen. We all have our fingers crossed that we can be back together at Westonbirt soon.

Mrs Bridget Bomford Life continues to be extremely busy – it's amazing how long it takes to do things properly!

A lot of my time is taken up with long-distance caring for my elderly mum, which, until COVID-19 hit, meant spending one week in every four down with her in Cornwall (a drive of over six hours, excluding stops!) Back home, there is always so much to do behind the scenes, so to speak, to keep all the care and welfare support running smoothly for her. At the moment, because of COVID-19, she is temporarily in a care home because home care isn't possible, but I'm very concerned because the home has a confirmed case of the virus, and families are unable to even speak to their elderly relatives on the phone, which is very hard.

As for Steve and I and our little plot of land, we are slowly making progress! Steve has fitted out his new workshop, and we've just put the finishing touches to my greenhouse, and I'm hoping to have seeds in by the end of the week... We continue to be delighted by all the birds and other wildlife here, and we now have a cock pheasant (Mr P) who considers our half-acre his territory, defending it and his six wives very ferociously if another Mr P dares to come near! Our own Mr P and one of his wives will now eat out of our hands, and, although common, they are incredibly beautiful birds when you take the time to look closely – such iridescence!

At the moment, the coronavirus lockdown is ongoing, and so far, we are doing OK. Steve has been working from home since October 2017, so is well used to that! A lot of his foreign trips were cancelled, but he's not too upset by this(!) and I suspect they will just be rescheduled in due course.

We are so thankful that we live where we do, and can carry on with our daily hour of Nordic walking from our door – it includes a section along the canal towpath, which is beautiful, and yesterday I saw the first mallard ducklings of the season!

Wishing everyone all the very best – keep safe and well.

Miss Valerie Byrom-Taylor Valerie hosted a wonderful reunion at her home in July last year (2019). **Patricia John** (Section 44) sent some lovely photographs of the occasion and wrote that it was 'a wonderful reunion… We had a wonderful sunny day in her garden, a delicious lunch, and an incredible reunion of Westonbirt girls across the years. Valerie made a beautiful cake with all our names around it and we each received a beautiful drinks mat made of silver (by Valerie) with our name on it and the school symbol, the amaryllis… Huge thanks to Valerie for hosting a great day enjoyed by all'.

*(**Editor's note**: These beautiful photographs will be included in the material we will put together next year, as part of the delayed celebration of the Association's 90th anniversary).*

Mrs Diana Challis Diana was at the reunion with Valerie and goes on to say: 'I have enjoyed another busy year with my usual activities at Westonbirt Arboretum, involvement with Tetbury Church, doing historic tours of Westonbirt House and visiting my cottage in Yorkshire.

I had a most interesting and unusual Christmas this year, spending it with my niece who now lives in Savannah, Georgia, USA. The weather was like a good English summer and we spent time on the Savannah River spotting dolphins and looking for alligators! A short trip into Florida took to us to Saint Augustine, America's oldest city. Christmas is celebrated on Christmas Eve, and Christmas Day was an excursion to a safari park. I had never visited this part of America, with many reminders of the slave trade portrayed in excellent museums. It was a real experience in so many ways. The east coast of America is very flat and prone to flooding, little did I know I should return to such floods here, so glad Tetbury is a hilltop town!'

Mrs Dee Francis I keep in touch with Dee and she sends greetings from Chepstow in Monmouthshire, South Wales, as follows: 'We are really enjoying life here as the Wye Valley is so beautiful. We are still very near Gloucestershire, so able to keep in touch with old friends. We went to Martinique in January which was lovely, with a stop off in Paris and Versailles. Great to escape the winter and enjoy the sunshine. Wishing everyone at Westonbirt happy days ahead!'

Mrs Mary Henderson Life continues happily enough in Bath, and it is hard to realise that seven years have passed since I left Westonbirt!

Highlights this past year have been a visit to South East India and Kerala with a group from Bath Abbey, completing the Hebridean Way with Chris Lloyd and Angelika Stredwick and organising a concert tour to Porto for our choir, Paragon Singers.

I am looking forward to playing golf on the Isle of Man with **Sue Cole**, **Sarah Nannestad** and **Sheila Urquhart** and accompanying St Martin's Episcopal Church Choir, Houston, on their French tour, with concerts in Paris, Chartres, and Bayeux. The 90th birthday of the Westonbirt Association promises to be a great celebration and I hope that many will want to join in the fun! *(Editor's note: As you will know by now, the celebrations in May could not take place, but have been re-scheduled for Saturday 22nd May 2021).*

It is wonderful to see the surge in numbers at Westonbirt and the success of the strategy to go mixed!

Memories of my time at WB:

The view from my study window, watching lacrosse matches on Saturday afternoons, ever improving standards in concerts and plays and wonderfully varied and uplifting Chapel services led by Mr Dixon! I loved knowing everyone well: girls; teachers; housemistresses and support staff and feeling part of the very special family that is Westonbirt. Of course, I will always be proud of the academic achievements of the girls which went from strength to strength.

Mrs Gillian Hylson-Smith I am still alive and enjoying Bath very much. It seems a long time ago we exchanged central London living for deepest Gloucestershire, but life makes us all somewhat flexible and I did learn to appreciate country living, though the sound of foxes squealing always made me shudder! What I remember about Westonbirt was the caring nature of it all, the pulling together when times were tough like when a member of staff drowned in the lake, or a treasured dog died, and the sense of family these events engendered. The support of Study One in running the school was much appreciated. Perhaps nostalgia makes us forget the worst bits, but I do look back with gratitude, I promise!

Mrs Mary Phillips I am still teaching at Westonbirt, although at the moment we are working remotely because of COVID-19. This summer, when I retire again, will mark a thirty-five-year association with the school and teaching for thirty-two of those years. My own memories are full of the many lovely people who have worked here and those who still do. There are so many wonderful girls through the years and great parents. The summer art exhibition is always a highlight for me and, of course, the trips abroad, ranging from Florence, Paris, and New York to Liverpool!

My family continues to grow, and I spend as much time as I can with my six grandchildren. We are hoping to get a Westie puppy this summer as our family doesn't seem to be complete without a dog. It is almost a year since we lost Shankly after sixteen years...

Rob and I still enjoy our travels abroad which usually means Italy, our favourite place, as we love the art, food, wine, music, and sunshine. Sadly, not to be this year because of the virus. I have missed teaching my adult group because of being back at school and I look forward to getting back to this group of friends and teaching art.

Mrs Helen Price Helen replied to the request for memories by saying: 'I think there are two things I remember. Firstly, the Roman Days we held, with 'chariot' racing on Piccadilly, then on the grass for safety reasons, the Ermine Street Guard firing a ballista over the lacrosse pitch, and a little boy next to me breathing 'Wow'. The other is the pleasure the Guides had using the grounds for their activities - campfire cooking, tracking games, scavenger hunts, map reading etc.'

Helen sends her regards to anyone who remembers her.

Debbie Young I always say one never really leaves Westonbirt, and it was a joy to return to Westonbirt just before lockdown to talk to the Key Stage 3 girls and boys about writing. One of the days I was there was World Book Day, and the fancy dress donned by staff and girls alike was as creative and entertaining as you'd expect from WB, including three Jesuses!

Life continues to be very busy for me, with two new novels out so far in 2020 (*Murder Your Darlings*, the sixth in my Sophie Sayers Village Mysteries series, and *Stranger at St Bride's*, the second in my St Bride's School series). I also released a short novella inspired by the girls knitting blanket squares at Westonbirt: *The Natter of Knitters*. In March I was thrilled to have my first St Bride's book, *Secrets at St Bride's*, shortlisted for the prestigious Selfies Award, which recognises the best independently published fiction in the UK.

Another Westonbirt connection arose out of the blue when former school nurse **Cathy York** contacted me to say she and her husband Gideon were starting a new venture in Wotton-under-Edge, taking over the bookshop in the high street. They have now completely refurbished it and it looks terrific. They will be reopening the Cotswold Book Room from the August bank holiday, so if you're in Wotton, do go and visit – she'd be delighted to see familiar faces from Westonbirt!

Like the Association's 90th birthday celebrations, the annual lit fest that I run in my home village of Hawkesbury Upton has had to be postponed till 2021, as has our village show (the second longest-running in the country!), but I am sure there will be so much to look forward to in the new year.

My daughter Laura is now 17 and studying for A Levels in English, History and Sociology. My husband Gordon is keeping busy in the garden. His latest project is to build me a writing hut!

If anyone would like to know more about my books and writing events, you can find out all about them and read the opening chapters of each book at my website: www.authordebbieyoung.com.

Section 88 (2019)

Section Representative:
Natia Jikia

It was very exciting to hear the fantastic news that you had to share!

Katie Battishill wrote to say that she is currently living and working in Queenstown, New Zealand – teaching swimming at the local primary school. She says: 'Had a wild journey so far, for anybody who has always wanted to travel and haven't ticked it off the bucket list... just go! Heading back to the UK for the summer before hopefully flying out to Greece for some more swim coaching.' Katie is also planning to visit France for a ski season with her sister **Suzanna Battishill** (Section 86).

Molly Bond is working as a PE teaching assistant at Westonbirt School. She wrote that she is planning to go travelling to Canada and then go to the University of Loughborough in September.

Lilian Chan said she is studying business management at the University of Hertfordshire. In her first year of university she already adapted to the new environment very well.

Lucy Featherston wrote 'I am currently self-employed as a groom at a small livery/hunt yard. Travelling and volunteering in my gap year with the hopes of joining the Royal Navy at the beginning of 2021.'

Izzy Griffiths is on a gap year. Was in Spain for three months, is visiting Australia at the moment and then is going to New Zealand and Singapore to make the most of her gap year before going to university in September.

Natia Jikia Currently attending Cass Business School studying accounting and finance. Very much enjoying living in London, made lots of new friends and looking forward to what the future holds.

Manaho Ogonuki is studying international business management at the University of Greenwich. Enjoying her time in London with new friends.

Cyllene Wu wrote that she is studying food science and nutrition at the University of Nottingham. Even though Nottingham is a completely new place for her, she has become familiar with the surroundings and adapted quite well to the new environment. She is very much enjoying her time at the university and has made lots of new friends. Alongside that, she joined the music society as a pianist and performed at the Christmas concert very successfully. She is preparing for some more concerts coming up in the next few months.

Section 87 (2018)
Section Representative:
Georgina Billingham

No news returned this year

Section 86 (2017)
Section Representative:
Thea Montanaro

Suzie Battishill Have had a very busy but fun last year at uni. I have continued getting involved within the lax club and I am looking forward to finishing in April. I don't have anything set in stone after graduating but I am hopefully going travelling with **Sophia Rossi**, and then a ski season with my sister **(Katie)** while also continuing to develop work in the TV industry.

Cordelia Cross I'm now nearing the end of my time at uni; I've had such a blast at Solent, and living in Southampton has been amazing, I just can't believe how fast the time has gone. I'm looking forward to summer where I can finally travel and put my degree to good use, photographing places around the world. Sending lots of love and well wishes to everyone at Westonbirt. I certainly think of it often and the amazing memories we made there.

Lottie Dickens I'm currently on a ski season in St Anton as a chalet host. After having a fab season, I have decided I want to do another one next year and work back home in between.

Camilla Edwards After finishing at Oxford Media & Business School, I decided it was time for another ski season. So, I am currently in Switzerland, working as a ski instructor for the foreseeable future and loving life!

CJ Egerton Currently in my final year at the University of Bath focusing on my dissertation about the value a dissertation holds to students across the UK. Outside of university I'm running an Airbnb, content creation for a few social media sites and thinking about plans to move to Asia after university for work. Veering away from law and focusing on marketing and content creation moving forward.

Isabella Findlay Still at Oxford Brookes; I've done my art foundation and now I'm in my second year of events management, also currently working part time in the holidays at a wedding venue. In the summer I'm off to Bali to volunteer teaching English for a month, which will be exciting, and hoping I will finish my degree next year - just need to crack on with some hard work.

Kristie Fitzmaurice Enjoying my last year at Cardiff Uni and think I'd like to stay in this city next year. I've been working in a tough pub in the city centre but learnt a lot and really enjoy it. Been picking up a bit of Welsh from my friends and looking forward to a break this summer.

Isabelle Gent I'm still at Oxford Brookes studying music in my second year, all fun and games. I live with **Molly Smith** so get little work done to be honest. I did a lot of travelling last summer and hopefully will go again this summer.

Fah Kerdsinchai Currently in my third year studying environmental science and management with an emphasis on climate change and air resources at the University of California Davis. I'm planning to study abroad in Antarctica next December (tremendously excited!) and then another year in university. But post-university is a chapter I've yet to figure out. Stay tuned!

Thea Montanaro I'm still really enjoying uni life, and it will be bittersweet graduating this summer and leaving Nottingham. Currently all my time is devoted to focusing on my dissertation on rescue dogs. No plans for next year yet but definitely want a break, so will probably do some travelling.

Jessie Padday I'm currently in my first year at Plymouth College of Art studying costume production. I am working as an intern with Dorset Opera Company over the summer and producing my own fashion collection in my spare time.

Emily Pearn Since we last spoke, I've been working in Bermuda for six months as part of my degree in international hospitality management at Oxford Brookes. Honestly, I had the absolute time of my life, it's crazy that I was out there for six months on this small island in the Atlantic. It was the most invaluable experience and a very humbling one. The job was tough at times, but I persevered. I am grateful for all the people I met, and skills I learned. Presently, I am working in London for Caprice Holdings and the Birley Clubs in the marketing department for their established chain of restaurants. It's hard work and very intense, I miss my beach bar, nonetheless all is good for me.

Sophia Rossi Well, this has been a big year. I'm currently on a ski season working in a bar in Méribel, loving life having had a difficult year with Hodgkin lymphoma. After my season I plan to travel India or Italy then head back to uni. Currently looking at Manchester, UAL or Exeter.

Emma Scott I'm now in my second year studying English at the University of York. We have covered a vast array of things, including medieval Arabic texts and the illuminated manuscripts of ancient Ireland (I think I may have found my niche in Old Things). I've really enjoyed learning Old Norse as well and have even managed to steal a module in early medieval music from the music department. I am having a lot of fun preparing my recital, and it has been a nice break from all the essays. In last term's production of *A Tale of Two Cities* my cello got a debut on stage, and I got to play the music to my own character's death scene. This term has also largely been spent preparing for York Shakespeare Project's production of *Macbeth*, in which I will be playing Macbeth. The YSP's goal has been to perform all of Shakespeare's plays within twenty years, and *Macbeth* will be the penultimate one, finishing finally with *The Tempest*. I was also in their production of *Cymbeline* last year, playing Posthumous, which was also very fun because we were in full Jacobean costume (*sans* codpiece), and got to learn traditional Jacobean sword fighting (the stage combat version). I also have my very own dog now, because I apparently resent free time. Her name is Pigeon and she is a Clabrdororgi, and her constant exuberance ensures that I always have something to smile about.

Kiera Segrave-Daly I am still at uni in Leeds, currently applying for placements with an upcoming interview for CSR at Disney, which would be amazing. I'm on the first team and committee for lacrosse, living with eight great friends.

Hannah Segrue Studying food production and supply management at the Royal Agricultural University in Cirencester. I'm halfway through my second year and start my placement in April at Relish in Cirencester, where I'll be helping source local foods for a market based in an abandoned prison. I'm hoping that this placement will spark an area of interest which I can pursue in the future.

Section 85 (2016)
Section Representative:
Charlotte Price

Sophia Ashe I graduated from the Royal Agricultural University in July and decided to go on a working travelling adventure to see new places, whilst learning about agriculture on the way. I spent four and a half months in Australia, split between working on a cattle station and an ostrich farm, and am spending six weeks cattle ranching in the Pampas in Argentina. Loving every bit of it! Hoping to return home to pursue a graduate scheme in rural and agricultural law.

Emily Brooks I graduated with a first-class honours in genomic medicine last year. I am now halfway through my third year of medical school, which means I've started clinical work. It's a little scary, but so exciting and I'm loving having contact with patients. I'm currently placed in Weston-Super-Mare General Hospital, but living in Bristol. Aside from medicine, I'm still playing lacrosse, spending time with friends and family, and training for the Bath Half Marathon!

Katherine Edwards I graduated last summer with a 2:1 in geography. I travelled the east coast of Australia then worked in a property company in Sydney for a couple months. Then travelled New Zealand and had to come home due to the coronavirus. Hoping to get a job somewhere but in this climate I don't think it's very likely.

Scarlett Jones So, I am now on my third season and absolutely loving life. I am currently in Méribel, working as a chalet host. I'm getting used to this lifestyle and have never skied so much in my life, the 3 Valleys is an amazing place for skiing, I have enjoyed every moment. Last summer I was in Corsica working in a bar and enjoying the sun whilst sailing and learning to windsurf too. I'm taking a couple of years out to find out what I really want to do for my career, and I can't wait for my return to see what is next in line for me, maybe working for a tour operator. I'm glad to say during this season I've used some of my Leith's cooking skills and have put them into practice!

Eleonor Parsonage I am in my third year at Falmouth working on my final collection, making inflatable garments for my final project.

Freja Petrie I'm doing a research masters at Swansea, looking at brain injury in female rugby players. I've started playing lacrosse again and still remember my skills from Westonbirt.

Charlotte Price Since graduating last summer from Falmouth, with a first, I have moved up to Cambridge to work for the university in development and alumni relations. I'm working within the events team and producing over 200 events a year within a team of eight. I have been working on my portfolio for events, with my favourite so far being Dear World, Your Cambridge.

Francesca Quince I've started at All England Lawn Tennis Club, Wimbledon as an estate development administrator and I am currently working towards Wimbledon 2020, so at the moment meeting all the players which is very exciting.

Jane Seymour (Allegra) Allegra just received a high 2:1 for her dissertation and is completing her degree (BA (Hons) fine art and art history) this summer. The Kingston School of Art Graduate show on the 30th May will showcase her work. Alongside her studies, she has started her own earring business which you can find on Instagram: @madebylegs(!)

Hannah Southam I'm working as a PA to the director of a local solicitors' firm and I'm also the office manager in the company. Have been there for four months now and I'm loving it.

Charlotte has contacted, but not heard back from: **Lily Cheeseman**, **Isabelle Corangi**, **Sally Gibbs**, **Madelyn Hudson**, **Hannah McKenzie**, **Eleanor Murphy**, **Hannah Reichwald** and **Trudi Seager**.

Section 84 (2015)

Section Representative:
Stephanie Thorndyke

No news returned this year

Section 83 (2014)

Section Representative:
Amelie Sievers

No news returned this year

Section 82 (2013)

Section Representative:
Abi Lowes

Saskia Burden I have now completed my last veterinary lecture after seven years of them! After my fourth year veterinary exams in February I shall be starting my clinical rotations as a final year vet student with the same goal in mind of qualifying and practising as a large animal vet.

Lucy Fenn I am currently the area communications manager for the Crown Prosecution Service London and think I have landed the best job in the world. I am also teaching yoga around my work hours and living in Fulham.

Alice Fyfe I am nursing and working in anaesthetics at the moment. I am currently living in Battersea with **Remi Greene**.

Emma Gardner I am now halfway through the second year of my PhD, and I'm still really enjoying it. I will be starting a lecturing qualification course soon as well. I will be presenting at a few more international crime fiction conferences this year and doing some guest lectures at university for undergraduate and postgraduate students. My partner and I moved to Bristol at the end of last year and we really love it.

Cassie Greenhill I'm still working in offshore wind and really enjoying it. We recently rescued a Labrador puppy from the Middle East and that has been keeping me very busy, as has looking to buy a house this year.

Aisha Gross I have just done a year managing a safari lodge in Laikipa, Kenya and have really enjoyed it.

Gemma Harborne I have just finished my Masters in vocal performance and song writing at Leeds College of Music. I have been very busy this year singing at gigs and doing recording jobs, as well as working with Leeds United Football Team on creating songs for their one hundredth anniversary video. I am about to start working with a producer on getting my original songs produced and released and creating music videos. I will also be going on a mini tour this summer at festivals and various venues, and working part-time at a holistic therapy centre doing music and song writing therapy, as well as meditation sessions to help heal people with mental and physical illnesses.

Annabel Jardine-Blake I am now working in adult outpatient psychology. I plan on eventually doing a doctorate in clinical psychology.

Abi Lowes Having completed the certificate in garden design at Sparsholt College with distinction last year, I am currently about halfway through the diploma in garden design and very much enjoying it.

Lydia Marshal I have decided to become a primary school teacher and am halfway through my PGCE. I am still living in Bristol and loving it.

Georgie Mobbs I'm still at Wirth Research (energy saving technologies) as a project manager, and feeling very lucky to still be managing our overseas refrigeration projects as I was able to go to Australia last year for work, as well as a few trips to the United States. I am also continuing with my HNC. I'm currently in the process of buying a flat in Bicester as well.

Laura Snape I will graduate with a master's in architecture this summer. I am still living in London and very happy.

Alice Truman I am now working as an accountant and continuing my training. I am absolutely loving my job and can't believe how quickly Florence, my daughter, is growing up.

Fiona Vincent I am in my second year of working as a junior doctor in Poole. I am currently part of the ear, nose and throat surgical team. I am really enjoying the job – it is really practical and keeps me busy. I also represent foundation doctors on a local, regional, and national level. I still really enjoy cooking, running, and living by the beach.

Section 81 (2012)
Section Representative:
Olivia Birkin-Hewitt

No news returned this year

Section 80 (2011)
Section Representative:
Emily Clare

No news returned this year

Section 79 (2010)
Section Representative:
Sophie Martin

No news returned this year

Section 78 (2009)
Section Representative:
Amy Falkenburg

No news returned this year

Section 77 (2008)
Section Representative:
Portia Ingram

Sophia Barker Sophia is still living in Hong Kong and working at Malvern College International. With the current COVID-19 situation, she has needed to change the way she teaches and has been working remotely for the past few months delivering virtual lessons. Sophia is thoroughly enjoying living in Hong Kong and has extended her contract for another year.

Mary-Jane Collinson Mary-Jane is currently working as a doctor at Bradford Royal Infirmary. In her spare time, she loves to explore the Yorkshire countryside and go on long walks. She has recently become an auntie and loves doting on her nephew and niece.

Portia Ingram Portia is currently living in London and working as an EA within the financial sector. She is planning on moving in with her boyfriend, James, later this year. She regularly meets up with many past Westonbirt girls from her section and hopes to arrange another reunion soon.

Rosie (Rosamund) Margesson Rosie is currently living in London and working within the publishing sector alongside many high-profile authors. Rosie still keeps in touch with many Westonbirt girls and was a bridesmaid to both **Lottie Mayland** and **Tessa Oliver** last year. Rosie is planning on moving in with her boyfriend, Josh, later this year, and will remain in London.

Lottie (Charlotte) Mayland (Sharland) Lottie married Daniel Mayland last October with a beautiful wedding that took place in Dorset. It was attended by many past Westonbirt girls, a few of whom were also Lottie's bridesmaids. Lottie is currently living in London with her husband and working as a social media marketing manager.

Tessa Oliver (Moreland) Tessa married Richard Oliver last September with a beautiful wedding that took place near Stroud in Gloucestershire, and which was attended by many past Westonbirt girls. She currently lives with her husband in Henley and is working as a teacher at Oxford Media Business School.

Section 76 (2007)
Section Representative:
New Representative needed
(Report from Jane Reid – Section 30)

No news returned this year

Section 75 (2006)
Section Representative:
Charlotte Boyes

No news returned this year

Section 74 (2005)
Section Representative:
New Representative needed
(Report from Jane Reid – Section 30)

No news returned this year

Section 73 (2004)
Section Representative:
Emily Paul (Stephenson)

No news returned this year

Section 72 (2003)
Section Representative:
Fiona Tubbs

No news returned this year

Section 71 (2002)
Section Representative:
Joanna Colson

No news returned this year

Section 70 (2001)
Section Representative:
Catharine Loveridge (Hallpike)

Amelia Annfield I am still working as a production designer/art director in London, based at Hackney Downs Studios. I have worked on some fun campaigns, most recently for clients like Hackett, Innocent and Nike. All work can be seen at www.ameliaannfield.co.uk. I have also bought a seaside garden flat in Margate which I am doing up ready for holiday lets in the summer.

Fiona Cameron (MacFarlane) So, for me this year obviously welcomed little Arne into the family. I've started working as a freelance jewellery designer and am really enjoying being back in the jewellery business. My second illustrated children's book has just been published, *Delilah Rose the Bogey Princess.*

Rose Farquhar Having been at Nyetimber building brand awareness and doing their marketing for the last three and a half years, I am starting a new role after Easter doing business development for the Belvoir Estate up in Leicestershire. I'll be living predominantly in London but up there when required.

Still singing tons with various bands and at many weddings and having a very fun time with it all.

Catharine Hallpike (Loveridge) I am still living in a sleepy village in Suffolk, juggling being an English teacher at Orwell Park School and looking after Rose and Annie – this usually involves doing a wheel-spin out of the drive every morning as we are eternally running late!

Tor Inskip (Jones-Davies) Have a daughter called Eliza who is now a year old. Living near Malmesbury, and working for Savills in London as a director in residential development. Eliza has swimming lessons at Westonbirt!

Charlie Murray (Smith) I am married and seven months pregnant and have a little boy on the way. Have bought a cottage in Lane End, Buckinghamshire. Have finished nannying and going to set up a childminding business from home.

Abby Warn (Moule) Not much to report as usual! We are still living in the beautiful Cotswolds. I have started a micro-bakery specialising in sourdough and run that in between looking after the children. All is well!

Section 69 (2000)
Section Representative:
Lucy Croysdill (Fletcher)

Laura Arnott (Griffiths) Living in Alexandria, Virginia. Really enjoying being close to Washington DC and all it has to offer, after Biloxi, Mississippi. I'm staying at home with my three children and have new admiration and respect for all of my teachers.

Lucy Croysdill (Fletcher) A shame to not be seeing everyone at the May 90th anniversary celebration but will look forward to hopefully getting together in 2021 to celebrate our twenty-year reunion. All the same with me, living in Tunbridge Wells, and my daughter, Nina, another year older (7) – time just seems to fly by. Keeping in touch during lockdown with weekly group Facetime calls with **Henny** in France, **Laura** and **Michelle** in the US and **Eila** in Hereford. Eila even dug out her Westonbirt lacrosse tour hoodie from 1998 to wear!

Rebecca Ferguson Living in London. Welcomed a son, Maximillian (Max) in January 2020.

Eila Greaves (Denaro) I've been living in Herefordshire for the past year while James has been deployed on operations in Afghanistan. The boys (8, 6, 4) have been at the local school and we've had a blissful time despite Daddy's absence. We're due to move to Aldershot in the summer when James takes command of the Grenadier Guards. I continue to juggle making bespoke curtains and blinds for friends and clients around the boys and now have my sister (**Alice Clarke** née **Kealy**) on board with the business too.

Clemency Jacques Incredibly sad not to see everyone at the anniversary this year. It would have been lovely to see everybody, meet children and significant others, and to hear all the news. From my end, it's been a busy year work and personal life wise. I am a counselling psychologist working in the NHS community and inpatient services, I also do private work as a psychologist and consult for various organisations. I've been managing a large team of therapists and supervisors in an online therapy service, which has grown exponentially in the COVID-19 outbreak. I continue to guest lecture on doctoral courses across the UK and present at national conferences for the British Psychological Society and Royal Society of Medicine. I live very happily in Kentish Town in London, where I have been getting very involved in community projects to increase green spaces and links between residents and community resources.

Veronica Jones (Green) The main news here is that we have a new addition called Rollo and he was born last September. He's my third son and Henry and Felix adore him. I'm still living in Buckinghamshire and working in the art world in London, but currently on maternity leave. COVID-19 has, of course, shut the gallery down for now, so fingers crossed we'll be able to get it going again. Buying art isn't top of everyone's priorities at the moment. Meanwhile I'm home-schooling a four-year-old and a six-year-old whilst weaning a noisy baby, so life is hectic, but not impossible compared to some. My husband, Tim, can luckily work from home for now.

Henny Vickery (Mercer) I'm busy chasing my two-year-old twins and loving living in the South of France. We have just bought a house in Opio so please get in touch if you're close! I am still teaching at the International School of Monaco.

Section 68 (1999)

Section Representative:
New Representative needed
(Report compiled by Jane Reid – Section 30)

Only those with email addresses were contacted. **Isla Richardson** acknowledged the AGM 2019 notice.

Section 67 (1998)

Section Representative:
Julia Collis (Bleasdale)

No news returned this year

Section 66 (1997)

Section Representative:
Katie Mason (Eves)

No news returned this year

Section 65 (1996)

Section Representative:
Catherine Hirons (Charlton)

No news returned this year

Section 64 (1995)

Section Representative:
Emma Lloyd-Williams (Leek)

No news returned this year

Section 63 (1994)
Section Representative:
Belle Morton

Bryonie Clarendon (Leask) No major change here. Boys are now coming up for 12, 10 and almost 7. Edward off to Sherborne next year. Events going well, concentrating on weddings, and sporting.

Clare Ferrige My boys attend Green Valley School here in Mallorca and we had a new head of secondary join the school in September of last year. Unbeknownst to me until a few days ago is that she used to be the deputy head of Westonbirt! Her name is **Judith Barlow** and she was with the school for ten years working with **Mrs Dangerfield**. We are both quite amazed by this connection, it's a small world!

Jess Ingham (Hipwood) Living in Bristol with husband, two kids and a crazy cocker spaniel. Working in international brand management for Orange. Planning road trip holidays in Ireland and Sweden, Norway and Denmark this year, if COVID-19 doesn't scupper things.

Nancy Lawson (White) Nothing very exciting to report but hopefully more adventures next year!

Mary McCarthy My only news is that I am organising a massive exhibition with Bristol City Council, running for five months from 4th June called 'Vanguard: Bristol Street Art: The Evolution of a Global Movement' at Bristol Museum's M Shed. The exhibition celebrates the instrumental role of Bristol in the development of British Street Art in response to the subcultural developments unique to this diverse and dynamic city. Vanguard present a display of unseen and rare works by leading Bristolian and British and Irish Street artists, with a special focus on international artists beyond the UK, spotlighting the growing relationship between street art and sustainability as we recontextualise the activity from its anarchist beginnings to the global phenomenon we know today. To coincide with the launch, we will be publishing a book with Tangent Books which will mirror the chronological direction of the show; we will be running a host of events in our Block 9 art installation and bar - film nights, outreach programme of events and much more!

Belle Morton Back in the UK for a few years working for a new American company and living down the road (literally) from **Sharifa**. Loving catching up with old friends and travelling to places in Europe I've not been before, but I won't lie, I struggle with the weather a little (#firstworldproblems)!

Jess O'Brien I'm living in Warwickshire, working in Leamington Spa for a third sector company, still renting at my dad's house (where I moved post-divorce) and it actually works quite well. We also have a lovely lodger. Enjoying travelling and seeing the world, just got back from Cambodia and Vietnam, but I think, along with the rest of the world, travel will be on hold for a while. So, in the meantime I'll be practising my credentials to become a full-time crazy cat lady! Still considering retraining, ready for my third career plan in counselling/mental health, but being quite indecisive about it all. Otherwise, hope everyone is well and maybe see some of you this decade!

Sharifa Parker (Taylor) Still working as head of people for a software company just outside London. My eldest started at Sir William Perkins secondary school last September and is loving it. Her sister is joining her this September. I'm sure they'll be delighted at the prospect of taking the school bus together! We adopted two more cats, so now housing three of the fur balls.

Section 62 (1993)
Section Representative:
Caroline Copland

No news returned this year

Section 61 (1992)

Section Representative:
Coquita Mills

Cordelia Gover (Harris) In the last year both my girls Jazzy, (11) and Ellie (9), have moved schools, but luckily settled in well. As well as my role as parish councillor, I'm now running our family property management business around Oxfordshire, which works well around school hours and their holidays.

I had a great WB girls weekend away in Swanage with **Lina, Charlie, Candy**, and **Sam**. I also get to see **Coquita** more regularly now that we live a bit closer, which is lovely.

Virginia Kelly I'm still living in Malvern and still renovating a barn. The children are growing up quickly and have long days at school, so I'm doing more work in tv drama business affairs. Have been in touch with **Coquita, Henry** and **Lara**.

Lara Masters I've been working on an autobiographical film script for two or three years which now has all the funding, but we haven't got the team together so unlikely to be filming this year, but maybe, at a push, at the end of the year. **Virginia** helped me do my original contract with one of my producers (for free) and she came to a script reading and met my current producer, who has given her some actual paid work, so what goes around comes around! I am still living with my husband Dieter in Willesden Green; it will be our seventh wedding anniversary this year.

Coquita Mills (Marsh) I don't know where the time goes but it does. I am still enjoying running around after children, but it does mean my annual return to the Association is a bit lacking in tangible achievement. They are growing. It has been lovely to see **Virginia, Henry** and **Corks** over the year and I look forward to the May celebrations at Westonbirt.

Rachel Terry (Pain) I'm still living in Hampshire with my husband Charlie and two boys. My eldest, Edward (13), has now just joined Radley in his first year and is loving it, but I'm missing him not being at home so much. My youngest, Henry (11), is now in Year 6 and is still at Daneshill prep school with other WB girls' children! So, I see **Issy Langley-Smith** and **Claire Warman** - they were a few years younger than us. I'm continuing to run my small recruitment business, fitting it in and around family life. We seem to be fairly busy most of the time as with everyone! Hope to see some of you in May at Westonbirt.

Caroline Walker During the last year, after leaving my role of child clinical lead at Trust House, Reading, where I worked with children affected by sexual abuse, I have set up my own private practice on the farm. In addition to my primary work as a child and adolescent psychotherapist, I have also trained to work as an equine facilitated psychotherapist, which means that I work with horses to help humans. Horses are very therapeutic animals to be near anyway, but when you add a psychotherapeutic level to the horse-human experience it adds a whole new dimension and can lead to profound healing. It's also much better for me to be on the farm and in the countryside and nature again, working with animals and in a profession that I love! I now have a herd of three characterful horses and hoping to expand it in the next year.

Seen a few of the girls over the last year. So nice to connect with friends that you know inside out. I've been in contact with **Sam Bowen (Neary), Corks Gover (Harries), Claire Galer (Dorman), Nicky (Rowls) Worthington (Rowland), Caroline Wilson (Pullin), Melanie Hobson, Candy Barnet, Charlie Haynes (Hunt)** and **Deborah Dereham.**

Caroline Wilson (Pullin) I'm busy - I'm always busy, and it never seems to change. This year I can tell you that I am still a farmer, a mother and a chartered surveyor which I juggle all the time as well as still running a campsite on the farm for events at Silverstone. A highlight this year is that I was made president of the Midland Counties Agricultural Valuers Association in February and so I have my own historical bling to wear with a presidential jewel and a silver gavel, which I am terrified I might lose - so it's locked up in my gun cabinet so I can hand it on next year! I am only the third lady to hold this role in 150 years, so I'm rather proud to have been elected.

We have a holiday home in Swanage, bought in 2018, which gives an excuse to escape to the seaside every so often. I think we live in the part of England furthest from the sea, so it's a bit of trek. I've seen **Lina** and **Melanie** this year, sadly no others. Life seems to be just flying by. My eldest boy is in his last year at prep school, so it will be all change again next September. Last September we moved the youngest to the same school, which has made the school runs a bit easier. Be great to see WB girls, hopefully 2020 will be the year for that? Still have my mum, so feel blessed to still spend time with her. Even though it's been over three years now, I still miss my dad. If you are lucky enough to still have your parents, enjoy them and indeed all those around you while you can.

Section 60 (1991)

Section Representative:
Rebecca Willows

No news returned this year

Section 59 (1990)

Section Representative:
Julia Roberts (Stubblefield)

No news returned this year

Section 58 (1989)

Section Representative:
Natasha McLeod (Marsh)

No news returned this year

Section 57 (1988)

Section Representative:
Fiona Stokes (Tobin) - (Section 45)

No news returned this year

Section 56 (1987)

Section Representative:
Fiona Stokes (Tobin) - (Section 45)

No news returned this year

Section 55 (1986)
Section Representative:
Emma Lack (Fitch)

No news returned this year

Section 55a (1982)
Section Representative:
Ouvrielle Roberts (Holmes)

Editor's note: The credit for Section 55a must be given to Ouvrielle, who has done an amazing amount of work tracking down members from her year group who, for various reasons, didn't join the Association back in the 1980s. It's absolutely wonderful to have all the news Ouvrielle has put together from these 'lost' old girls!

Our year-group had a fantastic reunion lunch at The Hampshire Hog in Hammersmith in July 2018. I am not sure of the final numbers, but well over twenty of us were there and many of us had not seen each other since we left Westonbirt more than thirty years ago. Following this, I discovered that only two of us were "official' old girls. As we'd left Westonbirt at different times, it is great to have our own off-shoot section so that we can keep in touch with the school and with each other.

Claire Coode (McCorquodale) I left Westonbirt in 1984 after O Levels and went to St Mary's School, Wantage (1984-86). I studied at Bordeaux and then went on to study French and business at the French Institute, London (1987-89). I worked at a variety of jobs before studying at night training to be a Montessori teacher. I qualified and taught for six blissful years in Clapham. I married a farmer from the Scottish Borders in 2001 and have two kids. I was lucky enough to go to the 2000 Olympics in Sydney, then the 2004 Olympics in Athens, and loved the London Olympics in 2012. Holidays are spent skiing and of course returning to my beloved Cornwall. Dad and my brother Ed (married with kids) are lucky enough to live there. My sister **Victoria (Tor) Coode** (1978-1985) lives in Hampshire and my sister **Laura Coode** (1983-1990) is a dual-qualified lawyer in Edinburgh. Both are married with kids.

Joanna Copland I am living and working in Battersea. Having taught and been a deputy head of a family group of schools, my role now incorporates leading and sharing the good practice of the group and also supporting the formation of a senior school, due to open in Sept 2021. My father **Sandy Copland** (Chairman of Governors 2000-2005) and sister **Caroline Copland** (Westonbirt 1986-1993) are also London-based and we see each other often. I am in touch with **Emma Bromet** and **Mary Rose Proctor (Bromet)** and enjoyed catching up with much of the year group in 2018, thirty-four years after our year group separated. A mini ambition is to go for a swim in the pool at the Copland Leisure Centre opened in the Westonbirt grounds in 2006.

Jude Reid (Shaw) I've lived in Shropshire near Shrewsbury for nearly thirty years. I have two girls and a boy who are 21, 20 and 17 years old. I regularly ride and enjoy most outdoor activities particularly walking with my friends in the Welsh Hills. I cycled from Bangkok to Siem Reap last November which was a fantastic experience. I have worked in education, mainly pre-school children, but I'm having a break presently. I have kept a close friendship with **Fiona Miller, Victoria Nelson (Sandars), Rachel Hinde (Davis), Sophie Gardiner (Russell)** and **Caroline Woodrow (Farthouat)**.

Ouvrielle Roberts (Holmes) I left Westonbirt in 1982 and went on to St Mary's Wantage and then Oxford High School. I studied music at the University of East Anglia, arts management at City University and then worked for the London Philharmonic as their education officer. In 1994 I moved to South Devon to get married and refurbish and run a five-hundred capacity nightclub. Quite a change of career path!

It didn't occupy me full time, so I also worked as performing arts administrator for the Arts Council South West. In 2000 my husband and I founded the Gro Company, the home of Grobag Baby Sleeping Bags and lots of other 'Gro' products. We sold the company in 2013 and since then I've been busy with family life (four children now aged twenty-three, twenty-one, sixteen and fourteen), some business mentoring, and lots of classical singing at home and abroad. I am now divorced, living in Devon, with two dogs and two children still at school locally. It was lovely to rediscover Westonbirt when my daughter **Lucy Holmes** (Section 86) went there for sixth form in 2015 and then stayed on for a gap year working as an assistant house mistress and teaching assistant in the prep school. A highlight was playing alongside her in the old girls' lacrosse match in 2018. My first experience of playing with a modern lax stick and boundaries!

Rebecca Whiteoak (Green) After leaving Westonbirt in 1984 I went to Oxford where I took the international baccalaureate at St Clare's College. Following that I then lived and worked in France for a year before moving to London. I got my degree in French and Spanish from Middlesex Polytechnic and then embarked on a career in television production. I worked for a number of years at London Weekend Television where I met my husband and after we got married, moved to Los Angeles. I've been in LA for seventeen years now. In that time, we've had three children, now aged sixteen, fourteen and twelve.

Sections 53 and 54 (1983-5)
Section Representative:
Sarah Clunie

Sarah Clunie reports that no news has been received from either section.

Sections 51 and 52 (1981-2)
Section Representative:
Lizzie Mobbs (Overton)

No news returned this year

Section 50 (1980)
Section Representative:
Lou Walker (Foord)

Antonia Doggart (Ross) I recently returned with Clare from a happy family holiday in Watamu, Kenya - a last holiday with my gang before James goes to Sandhurst in May and Charlie returns to his job as a guide in the South African bush in the northernmost tip of the Kruger. Clare is going straight back to her events company and I will be collecting Monty from his dogsitter, then back to life at the seaside!

I have chosen not to work but rather to spend time looking after and seeing family and friends while doing the odd cookery job and voluntary work with the elderly, both of which I enjoy immensely. I'd love to see anyone down at East Wittering at any time.

Astrid Mitchell (Sadler) Eldest son Tom got married at the end of last year, at Blair Castle in Perthshire, to Kim. Glorious weather – clear, sunny, and very, very cold. Kim is from Brisbane – her family and friends from Oz must have had a bit of a shock coming from 40°C down under to sub-zero here. They are now living just north of Edinburgh.

Younger son Rory is in London working for the Foreign Office. Life trundles along much the same for me and Alasdair. I was flying all over the place for the various international conferences we now run each year which, needless to say, have come to an abrupt halt. We have a publishing and consultancy side to the business too, but to what extent and for how long we can carry on without the conferences is an unknown. Or rather, how long this damn pandemic will continue and when things might start returning to normal is the unknown. Alasdair is still doing his farming and writing for the *Shooting Times* and is now a board member of the British Association of Shooting and Conservation. We also have a bothy (holiday cottage) on the farm to run but all the bookings have gone down the pan too. Happy days. Not. Although I must admit I am rather enjoying not travelling, and despite living in the middle of nowhere, we have a brilliant broadband connection so work is continuing, as is a major catch-up on box sets and Netflix.

Cathy Street Have just finished work as a research fellow at Warwick Medical School on a large five-year pan-European research trial and thinking about what to do next. After twenty-odd years working in children's and young people's mental health, I feel that maybe a change of area is called for. The last few years have been dominated by family health issues, in particular looking after my mum, but did manage an amazing trip on the Trans-Siberian railway from Moscow to Vladivostok last Spring. The experience has left me totally hooked on long distance train journeys, possibly next time across India.

Lou Walker (Foord) Am writing this from locked down Hampshire but am counting my blessings. My sports massage work is obviously non-existent for the foreseeable future, but health coaching continues as that's often been online anyway. My health coaching focuses on nutrition and lifestyle – sleep, stress reduction, physical activity etc – all the more crucial in our COVID-19 and post-COVID world.

I'm also an ambassador for the fantastic charity the Public Health Collaboration, working with GPs and other primary healthcare practitioners to help patients lose weight and put conditions like Type 2 diabetes into remission. Hard work, but, wow, when someone proudly tells you they're technically no longer diabetic after twenty years it really is one of the best feelings! Jack (25) is a science and physics teacher in Yorkshire. Charlie (23) is singing and being creative in Bristol. Simon and I are blessed with healthy families and a beautiful place to live in a lockdown. Love to everyone. x

Section 49 (1979)
Section Representative:
Fiona Merritt

Joanna Cobb passed away last year (20/11/1960-20/09/2019) and although not an Association member, she was in Beaufort until leaving after the Upper Fifth in 1977. **Myfanwy** and **Andrea** were able to attend her funeral and woodland burial in October.

Funso Adegbola (Ige) I am fine, as best as can be in this situation. Wishing you all God's blessings.

Mary Ashworth (Moriarty) Our newest grand-daughter, Jessica Verity, arrived safely in July but I wasn't a lot of help this time as I had had a very silly fall resulting in a broken right thumb and badly injured hand and wrist! I'm right-handed so life was interesting for a while. During that time my mother came close to passing, but rallied again. I was about to be discharged from physio in the New Year, but I managed rather ridiculously to have another accident - this time injuring my left hand and some ribs. Both hands are still under par but improving bit by bit. We are expecting another grandson in June so that will be two of each. We are looking to slow down a bit and Rob is reducing his hours; we will both stay in the finance side of the charity/church we work for, but hopefully will have a bit more time for family and other interests. We were looking to travel abroad later in the year but in the current situation we aren't making any bookings!

Cheng Sim Chan Happy to be able confirm that I am ticking along.

Neelam Christie (Gunther) It has been a mixed bag of a year for me and Jon, but the highs were good, and we did manage a few holidays. Madeira is an amazing place with a great climate - if someone wanted to live off the land in a quiet place, that's where to go. We also did a river cruise from Budapest to Amsterdam in November which is a great way to see many historical places and to take in the odd Christmas markets and Glühwein! I am still working in the NHS and, as you can imagine, it's been a rollercoaster recently: mainly telephone and video consultations as we await proper PPE and secure laptops that can access records so the admin team can work from home. Things are changing so fast!

Seonaid Coreth (Goodbody) Keeping busy, still involved with dressage, glad family and friends doing well so far and looking forward to when social distancing is a dim memory.

Myfanwy Edwards (Lougher) Sadly Dad passed away mid-February aged 90. He had not been well for some time, but it is never easy when they go. I now have three grandchildren with a fourth one due in March (Stop press: Bronwen arrived safely). Life here as busy as ever, still making cakes for four local tea rooms as well as the occasional celebration cake, although I manage to say 'No' more often than I used to! Time taken up with both the farmers' market, which is now weekly in Cowbridge, and the Cowbridge Food Collective, the online farmers' market I set up two years ago, both in an organising and producer capacity. Associated sites are www.artisancakes.co.uk and www.cowbridgefoodcollective.co.uk.

Janet Forbes It's been another interesting year, with lots of ups and downs (far too many downs, unfortunately), including several missions for work, mostly within Africa, with one rather interesting one in which the convention centre was hit by a hurricane. The roof was taken off almost intact and swept up, up and away, Wizard of Oz like, while we were still inside the convention centre. Some windows were blown out, others were sucked in - just as well I'm well-ballasted! Luckily, the host government got us to safety impressively quickly. I've done some great non-work travel, too, including gorilla trekking in the Congo, which was amazing, apart from the fact that I caught a terrible virus which I still haven't managed to throw off several months later. Gorillas 1, Janet 0. They seemed so fabulous at the time too! I'm looking forward(-ish!) to my sixtieth next year but am not risking planning a big trip until the world is more settled. How can we be hitting 60?

Alison Kerby (Wilson) All carrying on as normal, although 'normal' looks like it might be about to change with the current situation. My daughter is currently working as a solicitor in London, my elder son is about to commission out of Sandhurst and my younger son is continuing his farming enterprise at home. Otherwise Rob and I are carrying on our surveying business in rural Monmouthshire and helping out with the farm.

Joanna Kidson (Rowson) In recent months, the kids have been more settled than we have. Bex, now 23, has finally finished her studying at the Victoria University of Wellington - after five years she will graduate in May with a BA Hons (First Class) in sociology and a BSc in geography - and has started her first real job as a graduate policy analyst with the Ministry of Education. She certainly moves in a different world to the rest of the family, who are all engineers. Jono, turning 21 in July, is now very settled in Christchurch and continues his engineering studies, when sailing R Class skiffs and building electric race cars permits.

Philip and I are getting to grips with being self-employed. I have returned to the 'paid' workforce after a twenty-three-year absence, working for a firm of chartered accountants - who knew you could get paid for doing number puzzles! I feel that I get the best of both worlds as I am a contractor so can work when it suits me, and hopefully there will be enough money in the business sometime soon that we can actually start drawing money out! Philip has had a couple of engineering projects, but it tends to be feast or famine and he is either working flat out or capably managing the household.

Now that the kids are happily settled in other parts of the country, we have half a house that is effectively one big cupboard - so if anyone is passing through Taupo, centre of the North Island of New Zealand, do look me up!

Joan Lowton (Mullens) My new hip is doing very well, so much so that I have forgotten all about it really! Still working full time but hoping to cut down my hours next July when I hit the dreaded 60! Trip wise, we had a couple to Canada last year, including to the wedding of a long-term friend from my Ontario days, which was fabulous. We are saving up at the moment (both money and annual leave) for a trip to Antarctica at the end of the year, which should be amazing. We're expecting another great-nephew and great-niece, as twins are due to Ruth's youngest son, Phil. (Stop press: Maddy and Josh arrived safely). Also, my niece, who was our bridesmaid, has just announced her engagement, so all very exciting news.

Philippa Meikle (Main) All has been ticking along as usual; some concern now with having ME in these worrying times but glad to be in Scotland. Hope you all are OK too.

Fiona Merritt Both roles as aunty and executor expanded to three last year with the arrival of Milo over Easter for my younger half-brother, and my brother's demise in August. There have been many south London trips since, as he had been the main support for his wife. Due to circumstances and weather, only squeezed in one Plymouth weekend and a return week to Scapa Flow for diving but managed to include annual ski fix and variable levels of 'plodding'. Paid work finished mid-year (as no part-time option) with the plan to sort myself and home out in order to increase visits/social activities and assist with increased family help needs - slow but on-going progress on most fronts. **Marguerite Williams (Morris)** stayed over in October, when returning from a visit to her mother **Ann Nye (Morris)** in Cornwall, and we managed to tie up with **Nikki Tehel (Palmer)** for supper and reminiscences in London. All rather on hold now and hoping we all come through as unscathed and as quickly as possible.

Marion Minton I'm currently still employed, and the threat of a second redundancy has receded, so fingers crossed for another stable year.

Paula Palmer (Chin) I'm still in Basingstoke with Andy, now retired, and Rebecca, our elder daughter, who is saving to move out. Lauren, our younger daughter, had just returned from two years working and travelling in Australia with her partner when lockdown arrived – all five of us now hunkered down until we can make plans again. I was working part-time at a local library with no home-working option, but the council are looking at other options for us – maybe now is the time to consider joining Andy in retirement?

Andrea Radman (Beattie) Still limited earnings from teaching yoga but I enjoy it and it helps keep me fit.

Sally Scheffers The farm, myself and my 90-year-old mother all ticking along in general, but girding myself for the lambing season.

Nikki Tehel (Palmer) We continue to enjoy life in Dartmouth and opportunities to soak up the Devon landscape and sea views, more so for Wizz after his company down-sized. My role as the local area assessor/coordinator for Pets As Therapy had continued to grow, but I've just had to stand down fifty members and their pets (mainly dogs and some cats) due to current issues; the plus side is that the outstanding review of how best to match temperaments, and different requirements of hospital wards, memory clinics, therapies, care homes and school visits, may now go ahead. Tilly is not the only one missing the visits and wondering why home life/routine has changed!

Lucy Toyn (Phillips) Jonathan took early retirement just over a year ago so we have done quite a lot to the house and garden. I am still working, playing tennis and singing. The four kids are all married now: Graham and Chris both live in London, Jeremy has moved to Munich and Felicia is in Reading. We see them quite often and also visit my parents, in Taunton, monthly.

Marguerite Williams (Morris) I had four trips back to Cornwall over the last year where my mother, **Anne Morris** (staff) has now moved from assisted living to the dementia ward as she needed more care; we are still so grateful for the help from her nearby brother and her niece. Early March saw Jock and I in Seattle for his other hip to be resurfaced; weird to see the city and hotel get emptier and emptier whilst awaiting post-surgery review and permission to return home. Luckily my work has continued to be flexible and I've been working remotely whilst away, so should be able to continue during lockdown. David is with us at home, saving for when he can move out with his girlfriend; Helen is back to work, often home based, in Edinburgh after her three-month circus training sabbatical, but already missing her trapeze sessions now the gym has closed. So, it is now wait and see if – or when – we get the virus and no idea as to how long this might last.

Section 48 (1978)
Section Representative:
Amiel Price

Charlotte Harvey (Edgar) Generally, the year had been pretty much as usual - until January. I have taken on some home tutoring for students aged from eight to sixteen, mainly literacy but with a bit of maths too (Mr Clark would not believe it!) It has been fun getting back into teaching again.

Alongside the teaching, my work with Bridging Ages has been developing our on-line web app for our life stories projects. A number of schools have taken the project on which is great for the community and especially inter-generational interaction. We are looking to find ways during COVID-19 time to allow individuals to write life stories for their family or local vulnerable people, so watch out on social media.

Our eldest daughter (the circus one) is expecting our first grandchild in August which is exciting news. She and her wife are busy nesting and trying to stay well. Our youngest is in her PGCE year at UCL and has been loving it. She is applying for secondary art jobs to start in September. The eldest boy is in Hong Kong and planning to stay there for another year, whilst the younger one is working for a swim wear company (YouSwim) and enjoying the flexible working times. He and his girlfriend are currently living with us rather than in London.

Steve has taken on several consultancy jobs which has meant quite a bit of travel.

I see **Joanna Melhuish (Marchbank)** regularly and had been planning a quick trip to see **Zena Lunn (Marchington)** at their French house, but we shall see.

Johanna Justice Not a lot to report. I am having to have one chimney dismantled and tiled over due to serious damp issues, plus the other one to be capped and plastered before it does any more damage to the fabric of the building. Fortunately, these are outside jobs so they can still be done (during COVID-19 restrictions).

Obviously, we have no plans to go anywhere, or the ones we had are postponed until December. My brother's 60th birthday bash looks unlikely for June, so that will have to be deferred as well. I'm still taking the dog for his walk every day but keeping my distance. I don't work, hate shopping, and only go and do a shop when I really need to, so I'm doing ok at the moment. Thankfully, I have a garden that I can sit in and have benches situated, since before the outbreak, that are well away from passers-by.

Susan Kennedy (Sheard) (Written mid-February and before COVID-19 took off.) A bunch of Holfords (best house ever, says Susan) met to celebrate a bunch of sixtieth birthdays with a special tea at the Wolseley Hotel. **Angie Yorath (Haviland) Claire Staveley, Tella Wormington, Carolyn Henson** and **Nicky Morgan (Spencer).** We were joined by Angie's older sister **Margaret Metcalfe (Haviland)** and their amazing father Edmund who is nearly 96! I also keep in regular touch with **Rachel Dillon (Nobes)** and have recently had her eldest daughter Eve lodging with me as she settles into London life after university.

I am still running marathons, my most recent in Valencia which was a stunning city and run. I raised money for the Peace Hospice in Watford where a great running friend died last year of secondary breast cancer aged 52. I am five years clear from my breast cancer but still taking drugs.

This year I am planning the Stratford-upon-Avon marathon in April and Medoc in September. If I manage them both, the Medoc will be my 20th in 2020. *(Sadly, I suspect both these marathons will have been cancelled or postponed like the Olympics and everything else this year.- Amiel)*

I am about to leave my job after eight and a half years and looking for something with less responsibility.

Sadly, I can't make the 90th celebrations as I am doing the Green Belt Relay round London with my running club. Two days relaying all around some amazing countryside, minivans, medals and an overnight in Chelmsford! Such fun. *(Again - presumably not now happening but good news - we look forward to seeing you for the 90th Association bash next year!)*

Joanna Melhuish (Marchbank) No news other than we're all hunkering down here waiting for lockdown in London.

Amiel Price I celebrated my sixtieth last year with a champagne breakfast in our local beach-side restaurant with local friends and then dashed off to the Lake District for a week of wet hiking. Still very enjoyable though. My brother joined me, and another couple, and we walked every day and saw lots of rainbows amongst the mountains.

Earlier in the year I spent a different sort of activity holiday in Syvota, Greece, where Sian and I practised yoga, pilates, and had a go at stand-up paddle-boarding. It was great fun, but it was during the heatwave in June and just far too hot for me.

This January I managed to squeeze in a winter holiday in my favourite resort, Kitzbühel, Austria, where I succeeded in gaining a badge for my hundredth walk with the local guide. I've been going on and off for eighteen years. We took our own prosecco and cake, to celebrate both the walk and the birthday, up a snowy mountain with unbelievable views. This particular walk was with snowshoes.

I enjoyed taking my cousin and her husband around Westonbirt School last May for the reunion weekend, followed by a tour round the arboretum the following day.

Shame the Association's 90th has had to be postponed but I did have a mini reunion with **Amelia Trevethick** and **Sallie Robertson (Rowson)** at Amelia's sixtieth birthday bash in February. It was great to meet her family and friends. We also had a chance to admire her newly built home following a disastrous fire two years ago when the thatched roof caught fire.

Now in isolation (with the cat) I am working in the garden, sorting through the family archives, and planning to do more sewing since treating myself to a brand-new sewing machine that threads its own needle! Keep safe.

Lorraine Stanton (Martin) We have settled into the most wonderful village community and I am enjoying life more than ever. Celebrating turning 60 has put a new spring in my step. I have lost weight and now weigh what I did when I was 30! Living within thirty minutes of the grandchildren is nothing short of a daily blessing and we have a lovely space that I'm turning into a garden. I am about to embark on the Couch to 5K training (haven't really done any running since being at school), and to top it all off, I've just qualified as an independent travel agent. My timing on this one could have been better, but I will be focusing on the sustainable side of the industry when we get the chance to start up again. Get in touch if you are planning an adventure, or even a weekend away! Check Earthwise Tickets and Travel on Facebook or send me an email lorraine.ita@stantoncentral.co.uk. Wishing you all well.

Liz White I'm well and getting stuck into DIY at home and in the garden. Having fully retired from paid employment I was really looking forward to getting started with my new hobbies of photography and butterfly counting, but like everything else it'll just have to wait for life to get back to normal. Fingers crossed it's not too long. I've caught up with **Caroline Wilkinson (Winkie)** who seems very well and still enjoying all that Tasmania has to offer. Hope to see you at next year's anniversary!

Louise White (Smith) First of all, so far this year, I am doing well. Last year was not a good one. In March 2019, I had a very serious bout of kidney stones and actually went septic. The family was told that I had a very small chance of surviving, but after seven weeks in hospital, which included intensive care, rehab and then weeks of physical therapy at home, I was released to go back to work in August.

I started back to work in a different area of nursing. Previously I had worked in the NICU for thirty years, but I went back to work in home health nursing, where I take care of medically fragile children. It is quite rewarding taking care of these kids. It's also been a little challenging learning to take care of just one child at a time instead of three or four sick babies.

My mother and I are building a new house - not far from where we live now, but it has fewer stairs than we currently have - and we hope to move in this summer.

In the area of education, I obtained my master's degree in nursing, with a concentration in nursing education (MSN-ED) in 2008. I have taught in the local college, in their nursing department.

I have one son, Michael, married for fourteen years to a wonderful daughter-in-law, Carrie. They have an absolutely beautiful eight-year-old daughter, Eloise. (Yes, I am biased, but isn't that what grandparents are? And I'm accused of spoiling her!!)

I look forward to keeping in touch with you and the rest of the crew from Westonbirt.

Stephanie Wolfe (Binder) What a strange time we are living in. I imagine all the events at school will now be cancelled. My husband and one son are working from home which makes me very relieved that I go out to work in the great outdoors!

We enjoyed having ducklings and chicks last year, though we had to give our ducklings away as there isn't enough room for them. We kept the female chick who we nicknamed Mini-me as she was a perfect miniature version of her Aurucana mother.

We had a very interesting trip to Transylvania in June 2019, staying in a guesthouse run by a count and doing various trips out. I spent a couple of months learning a few phrases in Romanian only to find we were staying in the Hungarian speaking area!

In September we went on a visit to the Peace Village in Israel, which was fascinating, and we enjoyed a week of tourism in and around Jerusalem afterwards. I managed two items on my bucket list, viz floating in the Dead Sea and visiting Bethlehem.

Simon was in better health for most of the year but has since had a bit of a relapse. I hope we all survive COVID-19, our older son has pulmonary hypertension and is currently self-isolating in our granny annex.

Section 47 (1977)
Section Representative:
Fiona Leith

Fiona Dix (Bolus) Like most of my contemporaries it was the big year for me, reaching the grand old age of sixty in April - I tried to pretend it wasn't happening, but in the end, gave in and really enjoyed it! Had a few celebrations and took the opportunity to meet up with as many old friends as possible - **Leigh Ralphs (Davidson)** and **Gloriana Marks de Chabris** for example. I have also been busy working and travelling a lot this year. Working for Gillian Keegan, MP for Chichester, though the Brexit negotiations and the election was very interesting and compelling. We were not surprised to see her returned as MP in the safe seat of Chichester and I am waiting to see if there is a role for me as caseworker answering enquiries from constituents, as I had been doing for the past year in her constituency office.

I have also been project managing a defence consultancy start up business for an ex-MOD IT specialist. I have really enjoyed returning to the world of work but look forward to moving perhaps to something more challenging this coming year - maybe executive trouble-shooting, CEO's assistant or similar if I can find anything. Otherwise I am busy working on community projects in the village eg hoping to create a social/community hub, ideally incorporating some affordable housing, and helping the local small rural primary school become the first in West Sussex to federate with a neighbouring school rather than be forced to close because of small pupil numbers. My son has left home for Cardiff Uni and my daughter approaches A Levels at St Swithun's School with a lacrosse scholarship! How the game has changed since our day!

Katharine Hill (Cemlyn-Jones) I am continuing to enjoy my work as UK director for the national charity Care for the Family which, as well as being on the leadership team of the charity, involves speaking (including media) and writing. My latest book, *Left to Their Own Devices - Confident Parenting in a World of Screens*, has proved popular with parents and is on its second edition. We are still living in Bristol and are loving being grandparents to Ezra (8 months) and Evangeline (5 months) who bring much joy.

Cherry James (Lucas) Still working at London South Bank University, still teaching English legal system and EU law (yes, it still is and will remain relevant!) Still running and also singing (lovely Beethoven concert in the Barbican in March). Husband Simon has just gone part time, with retirement now on the horizon. Freddie is still living and working in Basel as an organist and harpsichordist, extremely busy with work in churches, operas, large and small ensembles and solo concerts mostly in Switzerland and Germany, but in the last year also in the UK, the Netherlands, Poland and Austria. Anna is still living about a mile away from us in London and working as a chartered surveyor but also enjoying volunteering for various food-related charities. Over the past year I have enjoyed seeing **Sharon Chen**, **Henrietta Ewart** and **Nicky Vollkommer (Sperry)** (whose wonderful English style choral services in south west Germany Freddie accompanied again at Christmas time) and being in touch with **Corinna Kershaw (Chown)** and **Gloriana Marks de Chabris**. Hope everyone is thriving!

Serena Jones (Walthall) I wrote last year that we'd had a wonderfully dry January and February. A bit different this year! We have only been able to do very light work in our woods in Herefordshire over this winter as heavy equipment is too damaging to the soft ground. We now definitely have ash die-back. Around 40% of our trees are ash, so it will have a significant impact on the feel of the wood if the majority of it succumbs to the disease, as is expected. Last summer we had quite a few thirty-year-old ash trees with no leaves at all and some one-hundred-year-old plus trees with definite signs of die-back.

We need to fell some trees to keep the footpaths safe and also where there are pockets of the disease, where the infection is spreading rapidly. Equally, we are hoping to find that we have some disease tolerant trees in the woods, so we don't lose them all. What to replant with is a big question and restrictions are imposed on Ancient Semi Natural Woodlands like ours. Oak has grown nicely there in the past, but the pests of deer and squirrel are problems they didn't encounter a hundred years ago when they planted our current beautiful trees. And we do have some beautiful trees: most of them are oak but we also have some stunning ash, sweet chestnut and yew.

I still do a bit for Westonbirt Association, looking after some of the older sections and also doing the content of the newsletters. I enjoy keeping in touch with what's going on at the school and with the others on the committee, including **Leigh Ralphs (Davidson)** and **Jenny Webb (Binder)** from our section.

I really enjoyed a lovely weekend with **Mary Wickenden** and **Wendy McWilliams** in Mary's new house near the South Downs last October. Those who knew us at school might remember that the three of us walked the Pennine Way together just after sixth form, so it will come as no surprise that last autumn our main objective was to go for a decent walk!

On the topic of being active, our younger daughter has just trained as a dinghy sailing and windsurfing instructor and has landed herself a job with our favourite holiday company in the Mediterranean. Guess where I shall be going on holiday!

Fiona Leith (Goodbody) At the end of February, when everyone else sent me their news, COVID-19 was still something going on in China. Today, March 24th, we are in lockdown and all finding our feet in this strange new world of social isolation and social distancing with almost all business grinding to a halt. They say it is only going to get worse for the foreseeable future.

Apart from that and four months of rain over the winter, we have had a nice year, not doing anything too out of the ordinary, just tooling along. Bridge, tennis, golf, gardening. A bit of work on the side. I did a lot of walking over the summer and spent a night with **Nicky Henson** while in the Midlands. It was great to catch up. For my sixtieth birthday we rented a little house in Herefordshire and had a very jolly week seeing local gardens and houses and sampling cheeses and cider with the whole family.

Many thanks to the regular few who send me their news every year. It would be so nice to hear from some of you others - do get in touch, you can get my email address from Rhiannon Roche at Westonbirt (rhiannon.roche@westonbirtschool.uk). If I don't have your contact details down correctly, you won't receive the prompt to send your news in. Also, I am looking for someone to volunteer to take over news collation for our section - it isn't difficult or too onerous and these days distance can be no object! So please give it some thought and get in touch.

Gloriana Marks de Chabris Still running my various property businesses – or rather my team are still running them while I ponder and evaluate new opportunities and make lots of mistakes. I have expanded beyond purely residential houses and am now looking to pick up some commercial units as less hassle (supposedly!)

I now split my time between Hampshire, where the business is based, London, as Graeme and Rosella have moved back to our house in Westminster (Rosella is at university in London studying PPE), and the North West/Yorkshire where our property focus is.

Saw **Fiona Dix (Bolus)** and **Leigh Ralphs (Davidson)** at Fiona's sixtieth as Fiona is a relatively near neighbour. Fiona and I also subsequently met to see if we could come up with a commercial idea for her local (defunct) pub – perhaps as a community hub?

I have had a recent email exchange with **Cherry James (Lucas)** as we hope to get together in London for a curry as we used to do twenty years ago before Graeme, Rosella and I temporarily left the bright lights and Big City. I had forgotten how hard it is to live in two places, and, more importantly, how to remember where your clothes are!

I previously forgot to mention that I also became British about eighteen months ago. Yes, after living in the country since I was twelve, I got a call one day from the Home Office asking if I would like to be British. Seems that I am Windrush Generation and they were terribly sorry if I had been discriminated against in the intervening forty-plus years. When I went along to Croydon with my various papers and documents, I was the only white person in the Windrush queue. When I worked for other people, I wasn't discriminated against because I came from the Commonwealth – I was discriminated against because I was female! When I became the boss, I could set a higher standard!

Tina Panton (Galanis) Nothing new really! Eldest daughter is engaged to be married next year. Younger daughter has graduated, finally, and now has no idea what to do next. We've acquired a new kitten; the other four cats are unimpressed, and the dog is just uninterested. I'm still trying to learn Greek. Really sorry I can't make the 90th anniversary celebrations, it's the season and I can't be away from my Sybil Fawlty work, Basil just can't be trusted alone! Hope it's a huge success and I look forward to seeing lots of pictures. Love to everyone.

Kate Porter (Bullock) I am now retired from teaching, and have had a few months working in a call centre to keep busy. Now I am job hunting again, looking just for something part time to keep my brain working and earn a few more pennies. Family are all well and thriving, so as usual much to be thankful for in life. Anyone is welcome to contact me if you find yourselves in this lovely part of the world.

Kathy Pratt I've lived in Hildenborough, Kent for thirty years and am a bit of a squirrel. I'm sure you can imagine the challenge I had getting rid of/moving all my stuff when I sold up in early 2019!

I now split my time between Hampshire, visiting my dad, and my 'new' (pre-1841) home down in Devon where I enjoy life with partner David. I've been visiting this village to see David for about eight years, so already knew many people and have joined several of the village societies. Since moving I've been busy with outside maintenance jobs, and commissioned work inside the house last summer. Now I understand why people with old properties often end up gutting rooms and starting again, though I've salvaged a lot. Just hoping the inside work will be complete before this summer.

Leigh Ralphs (Davidson) This year we have been focusing on extending and refurbishing our retirement cottage (whenever retirement will be!) which is on the other side of the Malvern Hills from where we are now. It has turned out to be quite challenging and I will be very happy when it's finished. So far, we have not had any flooding thankfully, but at one stage we would have struggled to find somewhere to cross the River Severn and the threats are still out there as I write.

Charlie and James continue to enjoy teaching, and we were able to go skiing with them over New Year which was a real treat. My mother has gone into a local care home after many years of living with us. She has settled in well and will be 99 in April!

I continue to take prospective parents and pupils around the College during term time and also volunteer on reception at our local Christian counselling centre. I do pilates and yoga a couple of times a week and I am trying to get back to golf (my frozen shoulder, adhesive capsulitis, is taking a ridiculously long time to get better). It's great having Monty (our working cocker, now two and a half) as it 'encourages' us out for lots of walks, whatever the weather.

As President of the Old Girls' Association there are times when I feel as if I am working full time! An awful lot goes on behind the scenes to keep the Association going and I hope to see many of you at the Association's 90th Anniversary on Saturday 16th May. At least the Executive meetings are a great opportunity to catch up with **Jenny Webb (Binder)** and **Serena Jones (Walthall)**. I also met up with **Katharine Hill (Cemlyn-Jones)** when she gave a talk on behalf of Care for the Family locally, and **Gloriana Marks de Chabris** at **Fiona Dix's (Bolus)** home last summer. Another (younger!) old girl, **Virginia Kelly** (Section 61) lives locally and we met up for a coffee and a reminisce about our times at WB which was really nice.

I still keep in touch with my old tennis girlfriends from Northwood and we had a fun week together in June at a lovely resort on the coast near Bologna. Guyon and I had a relaxing holiday in Antigua in April, and we managed to get out to Spain for a week in May and again in July with friends, and I went with Charlie for a few days in August. I went on a week's intermediate residential cookery course at Ashburton Cookery School in Devon earlier in the year in the hope of honing my culinary skills and getting some inspiration – however, as soon as I got home, I started to burn everything!

Nicola Vollkommer (Sperry) I thought that life was supposed to be slowing down at our age, but just the opposite is happening here. Five grandchildren have brought a load of sunshine and fun into our lives, we can't imagine how we did life or what we talked about for so many years without them! I'm writing my third novel, enjoying creating mean-spirited villains, naive heroes, and heroines who make stupid choices but are entirely lovable, and then making it all turn out ok at the end. I continue to travel the land speaking at ladies' events and enjoy two mornings a week at school. The Festival of Carols is becoming a fixture on Reutlingen's cultural calendar, and a wonderful regular opportunity to see **Cherry James (Lucas)** and hear Freddie on the organ. What a treat! Credits to **Miss Naylor**! This year, hoping to do Peter Cornelius' 'Three Kings from Persian lands Afar' - such moving memories of singing that at Westonbirt and always wanting to cry at the last bit: 'Offer thy heart to the infant King'.

Jenny Webb (Binder) Our big piece of news is our eldest son James getting engaged to Lois - a wedding in Northern Ireland early 2021. Before we knew that and its accompanying costs, we had booked a three-week trip to Australia, a trip to Florida to visit my brother (who also got engaged), a long weekend in Berlin, and accepted an invitation to a wedding in Corfu! The Webb balance sheet is looking a little under pressure now! Otherwise life continues in the same vein: governing bodies, tennis, yoga, singing, bridge, Westonbirt AND the family who are all healthy and happy so that is the main thing!

Section 46 (1976)
Section Representative:
Jean Stone

Clare Savoca very kindly responded to my request for news ASAP and sent hers the same day. Clare is still living in Geneva. She writes : 'Back in 2017 I discovered that I had Jewish roots, so I began a course in Biblical Hebrew, but had to take a break in 2019 due to ill health and several hospital stays. My elder brother died in June 2018. I celebrated my sixtieth with a bang in November 2018. I am now back to studying Hebrew, the historical geography of Israel and the Jewish culture behind the Bible.' It all sounds very interesting, Clare.

Jean Stone (Borritt) I feel very blessed to have had a wonderful year. My first grand-daughter, Martha Grace, was born at home, in June, to my younger daughter Aly and husband Alex. She is a real joy and now at eight months is developing real character. She is a very happy baby but thinks that night-time is party time rather than sleep time. I have generally managed to see Martha about every three weeks although they live two hours away. Once Aly goes back to work as an audiologist at Addenbrookes Hospital next month, I will be caring for Martha one day a month. I am hoping that it will be enjoyable for both of us! The family gene for red hair has reasserted itself having skipped a generation.

In September I treated myself to a late retirement gift of a bucket-list holiday. I had long wanted to see the Rocky Mountains and to visit Alaska, so I booked myself an escorted trip - coach through the mountains from Calgary to Vancouver, then a seven-night cruise up the coast of Alaska to Juneau and Glacier Bay. It was a wonderful trip and despite being late in the season the weather was generally good. I was struck by how clean Canada was and how friendly and helpful the people. Banff was a beautiful town, sitting in the loop of the river and surrounded by the mountains. It was almost surreal to sit in the hot springs, halfway up a mountain in the early evening, relaxing, enjoying the views. Our coach trip took in all the usual tourist spots, Lake Louise, Maligne Lake, Medicine Lake and the Athabasca Glacier. Although the glacier is still magnificent, it is tragic to see just how dramatically it has melted and receded over the past ten years. The same was true for all the other glaciers we saw both in the Rockies and in Alaska. It makes it impossible to deny climate change. The wildlife exceeded all my expectations, particularly during the cruise. I saw every creature on the dream list, moose, elk, bear, bald eagles, chipmunk, salmon, Dalls porpoise, orca and humpback whale. The icing on the cake was meeting up with two of my four Canadian cousins that I had never met. We enjoyed a meal together on the harbour-front in Vancouver, chatting and watching the seaplanes take off and land. (I suppose Harry and Meghan will be regular commuters on these now). It was certainly the trip of a lifetime.

Like everybody else my booked holidays this year are now in doubt due to the coronavirus. At the end of March, I am supposed to be going to Devon for a National Trust working holiday week. The plan is to make furniture for the coastal path, gates, benches etc and then install them on the path between Croyde and Ilfracombe. Most of the work would be outdoors so not a particular concern. However, the accommodation is in a very small bunkhouse where we would be in very close proximity to everyone else, so I am expecting the trip to be cancelled. I have also booked a week of walking in Orkney at the end of June. I will be particularly disappointed if that is cancelled but trying to restrict the virus is obviously of paramount concern.

I still enjoy regular organ concerts at Birmingham Town or Symphony Halls in the company of **Nicola Capewell (Wilson)**. Nicky too had a big Canadian trip last autumn, revisiting some of the places that she had last visited in a post- A-Level trip with other friends from Westonbirt. At that time, they even stayed with Miss Newton's sister in Toronto.

At the end of November, I spent a most enjoyable day with **Tanya Goffin (Sperry)**. I drove to her home in Leicestershire and then she took me out to a country park, where we had a lovely leisurely walk while chatting and catching up. We had lunch in an excellent tea shop and continued to chat as we walked back again.

Section 45 (1975)
Section Representative:
Susie Younger (Goodbody)

Lizzie Bennett (Phelps) Working part-time (a couple of days a month) for a charitable foundation which I really enjoy - keeps the brain ticking over but doesn't interfere too much with my social life!

Dave cut back his work to two days a week last June and retired completely just before Christmas, so we are planning doing bits to the house and various trips away this year in between regular visits to my Dad (93) in Suffolk. Last year we managed breaks in the New Forest, Guernsey (where we caught up with **Lorna (Hooley)** and Jonathan which was lovely), Dorset, Yorkshire and Rhodes. I also had a great few day with **Fiona (Stokes)** in Anglesey in the autumn.

Dave, Emma and I had a long weekend in Istanbul at the beginning of January and I am off to Tenerife this weekend to meet up with **Jane Golding (Gaffney)** for a few days. Dave and I also have a trip to Porto and Lisbon booked in May. Now need to plan trips for later in the year!

Fiona Stokes (Tobin) Life seems to be shooting by. We are still in Bagshot with Matt and Ben living at home, though we don't see much of them as they are at work during the day and either they or we are out socialising or doing gym (them) or choral singing (us!) Ollie and partner Claire are living in Cheshire (Wirral) and he works for Best Companies (great name!) just outside Wrexham. I am writing this in early March and spending two days a week with my mum (90) in Oxfordshire as she was taken ill with severe abdominal pain in December and had a spell over Christmas in hospital. I lived with Mum for the weeks before and after her stay with the NHS, and then in mid-January went to Australia (see next paragraph) during which time my sister Nicola came and lived with her. Thankfully Mum has since made a good recovery, so I am back at home with Chris.

Ben has completed Leg 5 of the Clipper Round the World Yacht Race 2019-2020 from Australia to the Philippines (the whole race, comprising eight legs, started in London on 1st Sept 2019 and is due to complete in early August 2020 back in London). The fleet of eleven identical seventy-foot ocean racing yachts started Leg 5 in Airlie Beach, Whitsunday Islands, Queensland. Chris and I headed out to join Ben in mid-January, and managed to watch the formal departure, the Parade of Sail, on 18th January (though the race started out to sea a couple of days later than scheduled due to technical issues with 3 of the yachts).

We met up as planned with **Clare Williams** who was staying three minutes' walk away from our accommodation and waving off her friend Fiona (similar vintage to us!), who was on the same yacht as Ben! We shared some wonderful drinks and meals at their rental, some great meals out, and some lovely downtime by our hotel swimming pool. Ben was on two months' unpaid leave from his job, having previously saved up a small fortune to pay for his trip (the crew members are all paying amateurs, who receive the same four weeks of training over a two-year period prior to their departure).

He has also managed individually to raise over £1,200 in sponsorship for UNICEF with whom the Clipper Race is in partnership. (Thanks to those Westonbirt friends who have already generously sponsored him). To anyone who is interested, any donation, however modest, would be gratefully received and these may be made right up until the end of the race in August. Go to www.justgiving.com and search 'bensclipperrace'. I feel he and the crew of Punta del Este deserve every penny they have raised, along with funds raised by the crews of the other ten yachts.

Initially the yachts were headed for China, but were subsequently diverted because of COVID-19 outbreak. They were meant to reach Sanya, tropical SW China, then head to Subic Bay, Philippines, for a second shorter race, and thence a third and final short race to Zhuhai, near Hong Kong and Macau.

However, the three races were amalgamated into two, and the second race took the fleet up north in a loop to some of the smaller Japanese Ryukyu islands, and back to Subic Bay. At this point I had to get the atlas out and do some serious study. My knowledge of the geography of the Far East has increased exponentially!

Our trip to Australia was also an opportunity to visit Melbourne and the Australian Open, where we spent two memorable days with some friends from the UK who were also travelling around the continent. I would love to visit all the tennis Grand Slam events, so have now ticked off the one furthest away! We returned home via Singapore at the end of January, where we met up with two of Chris's relatives (a niece and a cousin, both working there) and spent a merry afternoon with a former colleague of his from their bachelor days in Buenos Aires. We got home just before COVID-19 was hitting the headlines in the UK.

Very sadly Clare's wonderful father passed away whilst she was still out in New Zealand. **Jane Seymour** and I were able to be with her at his funeral in Sussex on 3rd March.

I have met up during the past year with **Lizzie Bennett (Phelps)** and **Trudy Evans (Wardle)**, and have been in contact with **Virginia Mullan (Sanders)**, and had exchanges of emails with **Jane Golding (Gaffney), Bettzan Mar (Wing)** and **Ali Cheeseman (Dorey)**. Jane was sadly widowed last September, and around the same time Bettzan's adopted daughter (23), died in San Francisco.

Valerie Byrom Taylor (staff) hosted a wonderful lunch at her home last July at which various Old Girls were present including **Tish Bush, Jenefer Greenwood, Anne Millman** and **Gilly Stuart Smith (Ward)**. **Jen Greenwood** also organised tickets to see Enid Blyton's *Malory Towers* in October at the Oxford Playhouse. It was an absolute joy - hoots of laughter and trips down memory lane to boarding school!

Gilly Stuart Smith (Ward) I couldn't remember whether I had contributed to the News last year, so I decided to download it to my Kindle (very cheap at £1.99). However, it was not a good experience for me, as it was just not possible to flick through a Kindle and pick out the interesting articles/years/people as you would do with a hard copy. So, this year, I will be buying the real thing! And no, I hadn't contributed!

Last summer I went with **Davina Instone (Vetch)** to one of **Miss Byrom Taylor's** garden parties near Newbury where it was fun to see so many old faces, among them **Anne Millman, Ali Dorey**, **Tish Bush, Carol Cleal** and **Carol Kynnersley**. We have also been to the Chalke Valley History Festival in June for the last two years, where we bump into **Fiona Leith (Goodbody)** and Charlie.

This New Year we went to Oman for two weeks and travelled from Musandam in the north to Salalah in the south, also including the wonderful Nizwa Goat Fair, the desert, and finally Muscat. It was my first trip to the Arabian Peninsula and quite a geography lesson, as well as a cultural one. Then two days after we returned, the amazing Sultan Qaboos died after nearly fifty years of steering the country on a course of complete modernisation whilst maintaining a neutral stance in an otherwise volatile area.

Susie Younger (Goodbody) I am a grandmother at last which is thrilling – Alfred, aged two months. They are coming to live with us in a few weeks while the house they have bought near us has a massive amount of work done, so I think they will be us for some time. It will be lovely to get to know him. Slightly worried about his poor mother having to put up with her in-laws with a small baby!

We have nearly finished our holiday cottage project on the west of Scotland and are finally ready to market it just as the country closes down for business. We will fortunately be able to enjoy it ourselves!

I hope everyone stays well, and fingers crossed that we get through this thing soon.

Section 44 (1974)
Section Representative:
Elizabeth Battye (Jones)

Elizabeth Battye (Jones) Our main family news this year is that our son got married in September. We all had a lovely family day in Norfolk for his wedding. I am also grandmother to Edward (16 months), my daughter's son. It is wonderful to see how much he develops and so quickly. I am enjoying retirement and have taken up some voluntary work as well as participating in a history group and various walking groups.

Jennifer Denholm (Goodbody) Jenny says she moved house just before Christmas and on Christmas Day itself had all her daughters and their families there, including five tiny grandchildren all under the age of 3, which was very exciting!

Pauline Jackson (Garrett) No globe-trotting for me in the last twelve months. Just share my time between my home in the UK and the villa in Spain. Always lots to do to keep me busy. Playing tennis as a means to try and get fit! Have bought a piano - have not played since school - so somewhat rusty to say the least! I have been learning Spanish for the past couple of years and I took my Spanish GCSE - A*!

Oldest son Stephen, electrician, lives in Spain and works mainly in Holland and Germany. Son Paul, cinematographer, lives in London, as does Laura, film and programme producer. Youngest son David lives with me, along with his two North American Akitas.

I see **Felicia Milicevic (Leman)** on occasion and play Scrabble with **Charlotte England (Wren)** on a daily basis, on-line.

Margaret Miller Brown I felt quite lucky to have had two trips to the UK this past year, one of which included a trip to Westonbirt. We stayed in a lovely apartment in Tetbury called The Surveyor's House, which I highly recommend, and managed to take a tour of Westonbirt on one of the few days that the house is open to the public. I had been telling my husband and sons about our school but suffering from a nagging sense of impostor's syndrome: had I really gone to a school as grand as that or was my memory playing tricks on me? From the sceptical looks on my family's faces, I was afraid I had set them up for disappointment. All that changed, however, when we actually got to Westonbirt and their collective jaws dropped. In fact, it was even more impressive than I had remembered it. It was wonderful to go back as an adult and really appreciate the architectural details and the restoration work it must have required. The very knowledgeable women who gave us the tour taught me more than I had ever known about Westonbirt's history, complete with the location of Miss Newton's final resting place! It was truly one of the highlights of my year.

Section 43 (1973)
Section Representative:
Sarah Thomas (Leslie)

Lorraine Clemie (Gibbs) I am back working three days a week, plus we have four grandchildren under four who we have on Wednesdays and often at the weekend too. So not much time for sitting in the garden!

Miranda Godbaz (Stracey) I am now retired, and Peter and I have moved to Palmerston North to be near our married daughter Susannah. She told us the other day that she and husband Josh are having a baby girl in July. We are so happy for them and so excited ourselves to have a first grandchild.

John, our son, lives and works in Mountain View, California, so we only see him on skype most of the time. Last month he brought his partner Vishali and her little girl over to stay which was such fun. It was amazing to see John being the parent, reading his favourite kids' books to his own child, and so happy. You can't wish for anything more as a parent, can you? I think about those times at Westonbirt and have a number of photos of the school on my computer which regularly appear when I open it up! Such a beautiful environment for a school. Weren't we lucky to go there!

Sarah Hackett (Walton) Currently I'm one of those in education wondering if the schools will be shutting. Have plans to clear loft, tidy drawers, and organise garage in amongst practising Ethel Smyth's 'Violin Sonata' if it all comes to pass. Yes, all those fantastic resolutions!

Not a great deal to report in the last year. Making inroads into the repertoire for trumpet, violin and piano. Started with Eric Ewazen's 'Trio for Violin, Trumpet and Piano', which if anybody has time to listen to it is very engaging and was extremely popular with the audience. The latest one was James M Stephenson's 'Trio Sonata for Violin, Trumpet and Piano'.

Clearing through my father's old possessions my sister found a letter from Miss Newton to him. It appeared one school holiday he had sent me back to school with a report he'd written on all the schoolwork I'd been made to do in the holidays. Unfortunately, a copy of his actual report was not there but her letter back to him was absolutely priceless. Having worked as a teacher and dealt with awkward parents, I thoroughly appreciated her turn of phrase. I didn't particularly feel on her wavelength when I was at Westonbirt, but had absolutely no idea this was going on in the background whilst I was there, so she shot up hugely in my estimation. I bet no other Headmistress or Headmaster since has been sent a report on a child by a parent. Three cheers for Miss Newton.

Nearly went to see **Maryon** last Summer but a flat battery in the TVR precluded that. The AA got us started in Minehead and we didn't dare stop anywhere except at Haynes Motor Museum for lunch and then home. We reasoned that Haynes would be able to give us a further jump start if needed.

Been out litter picking yesterday as council will not clear our unmade road. Now anybody quarantined inside will be able to look out on litter free view.

Best wishes to everybody. Hopefully, none of us will fall off our perches, but if we do then it was lovely knowing you all.

Maryon Jeane (Howard) Devon is super and the house is far easier to manage (as is the garden) than at Juniper Cottage. The weather is also balmier and, best of all perhaps, we're only a skip and a jump away from the sea - I can actually get to the sea on my (electric) bicycle!

Last year was a bit manic, what with the move (we moved ourselves, would you believe, doing everything from the planning, packing up, packing the moving van times without number, driving it here, unpacking, etc!), the death of my beloved cat Myrrh (over seventeen years with her as constant companion, night and day), the deaths of two close friends, and the acquisition of two kittens (Oriental Shorthairs, like Myrrh, sisters from the same litter). This last has, of course, turned out to be soul balm - but the process of finding them, getting them over the nightmare of kittenhood etc was not exactly a stress-free operation, so it's very good indeed to be in calmer waters now, at least for a while.

We moved because BT, in finally upgrading our small hamlet to 'Faster Broadband' under the Government's (very hit-and-miss, and still ongoing after eight years) initiative, missed out four houses - and, in the process, destroyed what 'broadband' we had. So, I couldn't work at all and Edward could only work out of house, which meant his being away from home very early Monday to very late Friday. Here we have just-about-doable broadband so Edward can work at home and I can do some types of work - but Gigaclear (who now have the Government contract after BT's failed and feeble attempt) are in the throes of implementing cable broadband here. So, fingers crossed.

Kok-tee Khaw Pete and I are fine. We keep in touch with our medical friends at university, and this year all of us were supposed to celebrate our 65th birthday in 2020 in a palazzo in Venice in April. COVID-19 has ended it though. My sister and husband are the same as us, celebrating their 70th birthday with parties galore this weekend. They are debating whether to cancel them. Also, they are a high-risk category for COVID-19. At least we find solace in self-isolation, reading books and doing laundry. Everything else is on hold.

Sarah Thomas (Leslie) I, myself, have had a good year. We so enjoyed our oldest daughter's wedding in Rhodes last July. The weather was glorious and the venue magical. I am still enjoying my job as financial controller of a Japanese company. We moved to a newly built premises in Warwick last year, and luckily this is very close to my home. We are still in the office despite COVID-19, but are currently setting up measures to be able to have as many people as possible working from home. I am still a keen bell-ringer, but this has all come to a halt with COVID-19 restrictions. Let's hope we all come through safely and get back to normal as soon as possible.

My sister **Jean Leslie** (Section 41) still lives in Australia and is retired now. She will be visiting for a few months later in the year.

Section 42 (1972)
Section Representative:
Miranda Purves (Saxby-Soffe)

We are all now living under the threat of COVID-19 but are still hoping to have a grand reunion in September. I have additionally heard from **Miranda Bostroem (Cumming-Bruce)** who lives a 'charmed life' in California with lots of dance and music and wonderful friends. Another American resident is **Anne Jarman (Weatherall)** who is sadly in poor health. LinkedIn tells me that **Gillian Haslehurst-Smith (Morris)** has now been 27 years at the James Ruse High School. Keep well, everyone.

Jane Barrett Nothing much exciting, I'm afraid. We had a nice cruise to the Med last September, and my husband became a great-grandfather last July, making him feel very old. The baby is quite astonishingly like all others. For now, we are sitting at home, ensuring we have a good supply of wine, which seldom makes things worse.

Libby Coats (Clover) says all is well and they are kept busy on the family front. Both their mothers are still alive, and they have two grandchildren. She has taken up ballet for the aged – a less likely candidate would be difficult to find (her words, not mine!), but it is a great laugh. She now realises how fortunate she is to be hale and hearty enough at present to do these capers.

Sally Gesua (Clifford) Absolutely nothing to report - diary empty! Taken up running again to try and stay sane but this will probably kill me if COVID-19 doesn't! Not seen anyone from WB or even heard anything. I do feel so very weird and don't suppose our lives will ever be the same again.

Miranda Purves (Saxby-Soffe) I had a wonderful holiday last December starting in Cape Town, then flying to stay at a camp on Antarctica, where we were taken out on (somewhat challenging) excursions each day, such as walking through ice tunnels, rock climbing and zip wiring, culminating in walking to the South Pole (well, we walked from where our restored DC9 plane had landed). Penguin watching, excellent food and specialised cocktails made our stay there very enjoyable. Now, like everyone else, we are all living under the threat of COVID-19 and all activities suspended.

Guilia Rhodes (Bartrum) is now mostly retired and only going to the British Museum one or two days a week in connection with a few research projects.

Amanda Ross (George) had managed to have a lovely weekend with **Jane Barrett** in spite of Storm Ciara.

Joceline San No exciting news to tell you other than I became a state pensioner a few weeks ago and got my Freedom Pass. I am due to travel to Singapore in May but unlikely now, so plan to reschedule for September or October, virus permitting, so unable to commit to dates for reunion. More cheerful news is that **Rekha Dutt (Ghose)** from year below us is in town from San Francisco visiting her daughter and son who work here. Sadly, she had to abandon plans to meet two WBs from her year this week because of the virus.

Deirdre Waud (Ward) Both her daughters got married in 2018, so moved into new homes, meaning plenty of weekend DIY for Chris and herself, and they are expecting their first grandchild at the end of April! Last summer, they bought a brand-new yacht and spent three weeks sailing it back from Stockholm. It not only goes fast but, unlike the last one, has hot and cold running water, a fridge, a shower and heating, as well as lots of on-deck gadgets for the menfolk, and she is slightly in awe of it. Currently she is just thinking how lucky she is to live in the country, have a good-sized house and garden to hunker down in and a husband she gets on with!

Section 41 (1971)
Section Representative:
Jennifer Cope

Nicky Currie (Penley) The highlight of last year was finally being awarded a National Lottery Heritage Fund Grant of £100K for a major tower restoration project in our church in Hitcham, Suffolk. It took three goes with a thirty-plus pages form, not to mention all the other information that was required.

Getting it meant that the £230K project is now taking place. I'm on a steep learning curve on project management in a Grade One listed building, as well as what's involved in restoring bells and the organ; it turns out ours had over 800 pipes tucked away inside its case. I'm learning bell ringing, or perhaps I should say I'm learning how challenging bell ringing is.

It was a great shock to hear of **Jane Wroebel (Wakefield)**'s death. (I only found out when I sent them both a Christmas card.) It turned out that Jane had been fighting cancer for two years but had not told many people. It was equally shocking to hear about **Mandy,** and thank you to those who let me know. Is it time we heeded the warnings about our mortality and had another reunion?

I hear from **Angela Neuhaus (Lowe)** - her husband is now the Australian Ambassador to the Netherlands. They have been incredibly lucky with both their home and her mother's home in Australia escaping the fires by less than a street whilst they were stuck in Europe unable to do anything. Their daughter has been brilliant looking after things for them.

I'm still working three days a week promoting farming apprenticeships, it keeps the little grey cells ticking over.

Ann Grundy Well what a year... Highs and lows, births and deaths... The sudden death of **Miranda (Dodd) Harris** in South Africa at the end of October was a huge shock to us all. Her husband Peter amazingly survived the traumatic road accident and is slowly making a courageous recovery at home. Her memorial service in Oxford, and subsequent burial back in her childhood home in Newport, Pembrokeshire, was an incredible witness to her life and faith that is truly inspirational. She is hugely missed. I still cannot really take in her loss.

We continue to live near Farnham, Surrey, and are now both officially retired! We are part of a church in Aldershot and I am on the voluntary chaplaincy team at the Aldershot Centre for Health, which brings me into contact with a wide range of people.

All our four children are married, and we now have eight grandchildren, all of whom are very special. They range from eleven years to two months. Apart from three in New Zealand, we are fortunate to see a lot of them all. I look after two of the little girls (Esther's daughters) twice a week during term time. My mother **Janet (Jackson) Briggs** is still holding her own, aged 92, in the same house near Lacock that she was born in! She now has live-in-carers but is hoping to get to the May gathering, breathlessness permitting.

We are so grateful for our continuing health and happiness, in what is proving to be a rapidly changing world. We still have much to learn...

Mandy Mac I am happily retired and enjoying my time Nordic walking and rambling.

I have been on a number of longer travels, the last one was in July and August. I went to Canada on an Explore trip: Calgary to Vancouver beautiful. I then joined a friend in Seattle, and we made our way down the west coast. We stayed in Airbnbs, and used trains and buses - Seattle, Portland, Clamath Falls, and ending in San Francisco. I really enjoyed it as I had never been to Canada or the USA. Next trip is Lebanon, if it's still on, then it's Antarctica next February.

Meanwhile I am at home or in my studio. I am making a ceramic tree for my garden that will hold bird feeders - I hope it comes out of the kiln OK. Life is good.

Section 40 (1970)
Section Representative:
Jennifer Cope

June Barrow Green I am still working at the Open University though edging towards retirement. I've been doing a lot of work on promoting women in maths using history - history of the gender gap and history of the representation of women mathematicians, etc, which I have really been enjoying. I have been lecturing in Europe and the US, and I go to Abu Dhabi next week. The second volume of my co-authored history of maths textbook went to the publishers just before Christmas – all 750 pages of it! And the first volume which came out in the summer of 2019 seems to be doing OK, which is just as well, given that the two volumes were nearly fifteen years in the making!

However, my biggest excitement last year was coming third in my age-group in the London Marathon (and one of those who beat me was an ex-Olympian!)

We had a great Christmas in Somerset with my sister Belinda, who has just moved into a lovely house in Crowcombe, a village in the Quantocks, where she has been living for the last few years, and which is just the other side of the hills from Pightley. My partner Reinhard has had a rather wretched year with a hip replacement that went wrong – the wrong sized bit was put in, so it had to be redone and he was in hospital for almost four months altogether. But I am happy to say he is now back on his feet (and his bicycle!) and we were able to have some good walks in Somerset.

Caroline Cole (Sanders) Douglas and I got married on 31st August last year. My new name is Caroline Cole. We had our wedding at the village church here in Datchet, followed by a reception at Eton College Rowing Centre at Dorney Lake. We left by boat from behind the Rowing Centre and headed off up the Thames. We had a couple of nights in a beautiful hotel up-river, followed by an amazing honeymoon in Cannes. The wedding day was really special, and I'm delighted to report the names of some old WB girls on the guest list! **Caroline Latham** read a lesson, **Katie Hamilton (Faulkner)**, **Diana Farrington (Broughton)** and **Lally St Maur** were there and my three sisters of course, two of whom were at WB: **Daphne Sanders** and **Virginia Mullan**. Douglas has sold his property in Fulham and my house in Datchet is on the market. We have bought a new house in Datchet and are in the process of building on to it and creating a wonderful home.

Annabel Kerr (Johnston) My life revolves very much round my five grandchildren who are exhausting but give me great joy! My daughter was posted to the British High Commission in New Delhi last year, and I had a trip out to see her in October. Other plans to visit with the rest of the family have had to be rebooked, but hoping all will be possible in September. I see a lot of **Di Gale (Forwood)** and as she lives around the corner. She has been brilliant in helping me out with the children.

Jean Leslie Jean wrote to June with the following: 'I'm still living in Sydney. We've had some shocking days this summer with smoke haze, but nothing like people in areas impacted by the fires, lost homes, animals etc. I think the country is in shock. We will need to make a lot of changes; hard to convince the old guard. We've been way too slow changing to renewables. I've stopped work now. The best thing: I spend time up north in Coffs where a friend lives, and also come over to London to stay with my mum and catch up with family. Very fortunate life. So, it would be great to catch up one day, and thanks for offer of a bed, but I am fine for that, my mum lives in Richmond.'

Shan Oakes (Jones) Bill and I attended **Mandy Dodd**'s funeral in Oxford on 14th December. Mandy and her husband and colleagues were working in South Africa when their car was knocked off a bridge into a river: a terrible tragedy. The church was full, with family and friends and many people from A Rocha, the international environmental organisation that Mandy and her husband Peter had started many years ago. Using our WB names, **Karen Fielding, June Barrow-Green, Anne Briggs, Patsy Seymour-Williams** and **Di Broughton** were also there.

Bill and I are increasingly desperate about the future of life on our planet if things don't change radically – and fast. So, we continue to do what we can to promote education for sustainability and sustainability itself through various means: support for local, national, and international projects and action as well as through politics. We are appalled at the denial of reality by the people in power, and very tired of people saying 'we don't want to get political' when everything IS political! We should be delighted to hear from anyone else working in a similar field: shan@voice-international.net

Section 39 (1969)
Section Representative:
Louise Dixon

Editor's note: *As Liz says at the end of her entry, we are delighted that Louise Dixon has taken on the role of Section 39's Rep. I think we had seventeen entries for this section last year (brilliant!), so we hope you are all well, and look forward to an update of your News next year.*

Louise Dixon I'm writing this personal update at the beginning of the fourth week of our national lockdown in the UK, so that subject seems to rather eclipse all other considerations. Whoever would have thought we would be in this situation? I've always felt that I was incredibly lucky to be part of a generation which had never had to endure a war which affected us directly, but now we are the (pretty) older generation who are coming into the category of being vulnerable to the ravages of this horrible virus.

We spend a great deal of our time in South Africa and were indeed there from October last year. The virus was very slow to make its presence felt and, for many weeks, we followed the news of the spread of the virus in the East and then in Europe. Yet, when you're sitting in the glorious late summer sunshine in Johannesburg, with absolutely no indication of anything untoward in your surroundings, it's very hard to imagine that your little world will be affected, so many miles away from the theatre of virus war. We had tickets booked to come back to the UK on April 5th, and we were nonchalantly wondering if it might be better to delay our trip back to the UK, to allow things to calm down and for us to escape the effects of the epidemic.

By March 14th, we had started thinking that perhaps we should head home 'a little bit earlier', so we tried to change our tickets with Virgin Atlantic to March 28th, but, in spite of the warm words we've heard over the PR channels for the airline industry, we were told that we could not change our tickets and would have to buy new ones. Ho hum! Buying a long-haul ticket at short notice is not cheap! But needs must. Before we had time to congratulate ourselves on our new timing, an announcement was made the next day that President Cyril Ramaphosa would 'address the nation'. Given that, at that stage, South Africa only had about 45 cases and no deaths at all, it was amazingly bold of him to announce a draconian lockdown - without the right to exercise - starting four days later. The ban included closing the borders to all people who were not South African citizens or permanent residents. It's at that point that you have to choose where you are best placed to be locked down. It was a toss-up between staying in a place that seemed relatively unaffected, yet has a very weak health infrastructure, and returning to the much more densely populated UK, but which has so much more to offer in terms of back-up to a potentially sick person.

Time to change the plane tickets again. It was still less than 24 hours since we had booked the second tickets, but... 'Oh, if only you had rung last night. It isn't 24 hours to change tickets without charge. It's the same business day.' So we then had to shell out a fair amount to change the tickets, on which the digital ink was hardly dry, plus pay £300 extra to guarantee exit row seats, which might offer a fraction more distancing. Then the flight cancellations started to be announced. It's difficult to describe how stressful the process became of rapidly packing up our house and ensuring everything was in place for an open-ended absence.

Even after we had checked in online and headed for the airport, we still could not be sure that the flight would actually be allowed to land in Johannesburg and, therefore, be available for us to take the return trip. After a pretty difficult process through the airport formalities, we were more than usually glad to fall into the airport lounge and help ourselves to a generous glass of resolve-strengthening South African red wine!

Now back in the UK, we quickly settled into the surprising calm of the rather more generous lockdown arrangements in force. We've resumed cycling after a break of two years and are tackling a prodigious list of jobs-that-should-have-been-done-years-ago. I am sure that everyone is re-examining their lives and what they want for the future, and I am certainly no exception to that. What the present home-focus has given me is a preview of what life might be like in the future, when age and mobility might conspire to keep me a lot more at home than at present, and I am finding the prospect very much less daunting than I previously might have imagined.

Through chance circumstances of work, I live in the very place that I was born, very close to Derby, and I am, for the first time really, taking advantage of the unexpected leisure time to explore the spider's web of paths and cycle tracks that follow the rich network of rivers, canals, railway lines, local roads and arterial roads that take advantage of the flood plain communication corridor of the River Trent.

Who knows how long we shall be confined to barracks - in full or in part - but on one thing I am clear: I want to look back on this strange and unsettling time as an inexplicable gift that, among the difficulties and challenges, was a time of personal re-assessment and a breathing space to consider what needs to be seen as important for the rest of what remains of our allotted time. That in itself would be a silver lining.

Liz Jubb (Grant) These last twelve months have been particularly busy (and enjoyable!) as my husband celebrated his 70th last autumn. Thank goodness it wasn't this year when things would have had to be cancelled. We decided to do some travelling and in May went to the US, spending a few days at Niagara Falls followed by two weeks in Washington DC. It was absolutely fantastic with glorious weather. I don't think we have ever done so much sightseeing, both in the city and immediate environs, and we hugely enjoyed every minute. A highlight was being in DC for Memorial Weekend where amongst other things 'Rolling Thunder' took place, when nearly one million (yes: one million!) Harley Davidson bikes drove through the city in honour of their veterans.

In September we went to Crete for two weeks and again enjoyed excellent weather. Luckily, we had a villa up in the hills near Chania so benefitted from the sea breeze as otherwise we would have baked. A car ensured we saw plenty of the west side of the island and the numerous churches and settlements helped our lack of knowledge of Greek history.

October was fully taken up with birthday celebrations when we hosted a lunch at home for Phil's school chums and their wives. They have remained a close-knit group and over the years we wives have all got to know each other so there was plenty of buzz and having caterers in ensured I could completely relax without worrying about a thing. We also spent a week down in Bude, as we love it down there, and there is a very comfortable hotel where we can truly relax. This gave us the opportunity to meet up with family (more eating!) and do our favourite walks.

Otherwise, we have continued to be involved with village activities, such as History Society, Camera Club, choirs, and churchyard maintenance, but of course as I write nearly everything is curtailed.

Some activities are continuing in virtual format and proving very successful but on the whole, I have to say we are enjoying having a much more relaxed existence. Looking back at the first three months of the year the diary was packed and it was quite exhausting just reading it. Let's hope that at the end of all this we don't revert to former bad habits.

Finally, I am delighted to learn that **Louise Dixon** has kindly volunteered to take over from me as the rep for Section 39. However, as she has only just returned to the UK from overseas, she could not be in touch with you before the deadline for submitting news so it will be just her and me for this year! The current lock-down for COVID-19 is still in place: a horrifying disease which is ripping through all of society and causing such sadness. I just hope that by this time next year there will be a vaccine in place.

Section 38 (1968)
Section Representative:
Chris Shaw (Morris)

Julia Douglas (Neath) The main highlight of this year has been the return to Britain of our son Bruce and family from Brazil after an absence of nearly seven years – both he and we are very thrilled about this, principally because Brazil is a difficult country to live in for all sorts of reasons, but also because it means that we can finally spend our holiday money going to places we would really like to visit! It has been a steep learning curve for them trying to find a place to live in London, and harder still to find a place in school for six-year-old Fred. Anyway, they have finally landed up with a nicely converted property in Sydenham and they are hopeful that Fred will be able to start school at the end of February. Amanda, Bruce's Brazilian partner, has adapted well so far and none of them are complaining about the weather! Our youngest daughter Mia, who is expecting her first baby in June, lives in Lewisham, which is quite nearby. Laura, our oldest, is still living in Oxted, Surrey, so we now have all three of them within an hour's drive of Sevenoaks.

John and I are both well and enjoying a pretty active life so there is much to be thankful for. I keep in regular touch with **Chris Shaw**, and we spent a very enjoyable few days at the start of January with **Judy Kramer (Nettleton)** and her husband John in Malaga, where the sun shone every day.

Diana Gale (Forwood) reports that a highlight of 2019 was the happy rescue of a hedgehog who had got stuck in their garage door. Simon and his team at the Leatherhead Wildlife Aid Centre spent time and effort saving their little friend who they've named Don Quixote. The event can be seen on https://www.youtube.com/watch?v=S5ofceENdmg and is well worth viewing. Di catches up most weeks with **Annabel Kerr (Johnston)** and is in touch with **Hilary Hughes (Moore)**, who was complaining that her Brisbane garden was so dry that most of the birds had left it, although Di is not sure that is the case any longer.

Alison Gauld (Taylor) Last year Jim and I, who do take life a bit easier nowadays, enjoyed a couple of Mediterranean cruises in May and September. I became a sacristan at my local church, and am vice chairman (chairman elect now) for our local Good Neighbours' Group which provides volunteer drivers to take people to medical appointments. I am also a Eucharastic minister at church, and take Holy Communion out to elderly congregation in their own homes. I keep up with **Penny Bysshe (Osborn)** and **Sue Bottell (Rigley)**, who is coming to stay with her husband on the way to France.

Chris Shaw (Morris) There has been a disappointingly small response from our section this year, maybe because I haven't been able to chase everyone to send in their news as I usually do! This was partly because we managed to squeeze in a lovely sunny holiday in Lanzarote just before COVID-19 lockdown in March. Then I had a back injury which was so bad that I found it impossible to lie down, and barely to sit, for about ten days. Luckily it has largely resolved itself with time. I have had a bad back since my teens, and often wonder if it started with a very nasty fall off some equipment in the old Westonbirt gym (now demolished) on to a hard floor, which resulted in several days in the San. Hey ho!

We had a wonderful trip to Canada last summer to see my Toronto cousins, then travelled over the Rockies on the Rocky Mountaineer train to Vancouver. It was a wonderful holiday, with lots of echoes of my Greyhound bus tour there with **Julia Douglas** in 1970 – just rather more comfortable travelling this time!

Now that we are all in lockdown with no prospect of any holidays this year, it is good to have some happy times to look back on. I guess that for many of us one of the worst aspects of being confined to home is that we won't be able to see our grandchildren for so long – mine are aged 6, 4, 2 and 1, and are changing fast. We have to settle for seeing them on screen or talking on the telephone, but it's not the same!

We are fortunate to have a lovely community of friends and neighbours in our North Yorkshire village, who will help us out if required. I know most of us hit 70 either last year or this, but it's still rather shocking to find ourselves described as elderly and/or vulnerable!

I am also thankful that I managed to see some WB friends last year. Martin and I went to stay with **Julia Douglas** and her husband John in Sevenoaks in May, and they took us on trips to some of their local historic houses - Hever Castle, Ightham Mote and Knole Park. In November **Dee Sichel (Ferguson)** invited me for a lovely long lunch at her home in Oxford, together with **Jane Fisher (Binney)** and **Janet Johnson (Plowright)**. My plans to meet **Alison Andrews (Morgan)** this spring are now on hold.

Love and best wishes to everyone, and stay well!

Section 37 (1967)

Section Representative:
Jenifer Davidson (Moir)

Sultana Al-Quaiti (Rashid) No news, but looking forward to seeing everyone at her house in Richmond in June.

Hilary Davis (Stone) I really enjoyed catching up with so many friends at last year's reunion at Studland Bay, where we had some beautiful walks along the coast. I'm looking forward to this year's London get-together and also the event being held at Westonbirt in May to mark the 90th anniversary of the old girls' association.

No real news from here. However, I'm still volunteering at the Ledbury Poetry Festival and we had a very successful Festival in 2019. Margaret Atwood gave two readings and also visited the local secondary school to speak to students who were studying her work – what a wonderful opportunity for them! Another coup for the Festival was the presence of the three living Poets Laureate: Andrew Motion, Carol Ann Duffy and Simon Armitage, who all read their work at very enjoyable sell-out events.

I hope COVID-19 doesn't interfere with all the gatherings proposed for this year!

Anne Collings (Watson) My life has changed over the last three years. My husband, John, sadly died in December 2016 after succumbing to myeloma. It was a particularly difficult time for my eldest daughter, Freya, who is a consultant haematologist specialising in myeloma.

On a happier note, I have four very energetic grandchildren, all boys, ranging in age from 3 to 10 so they keep me busy.

I am now fully retired but have taken up making full size carved Victorian-style rocking horses. Each horse takes approximately 150 hours to carve so I only make a few each year, mostly commissions. I am a member of the 'Guild of Rocking Horse Makers'. I love making the wood come alive and also taking my frustrations out on a very physical activity!

I celebrated my 70th birthday in February. My children surprised me with a weekend in Yorkshire and the most fabulous meal at The Black Swan at Oldstead. It was a wonderful gastronomical experience and a brilliant weekend marred only slightly by Storm Ciara!

Jenifer Davidson (Moir) I have been as busy as ever with part-time bookkeeping jobs, tennis, and other voluntary work. I very much enjoyed our 70th birthday reunion at Studland Bay House, which was hosted by **Sarah Ferguson**. It was good to see everyone, but particularly those who had not been to a reunion before. Those attending were: **Sarah Ferguson, Alison Boxley (Fowler), Cas Boddham-Whettam (Burkitt), Daphne Sanders, Lucy Fisher (Sadleir), Hilary Davis (Stone), Alison Parry (Sturdy-Morton), Sultana Al-Quaiti (Rashid), Ruth Precious (Richards), Jane Hill (Rust), Christine MacLaren, Sue Ross, Venessa Pugh, Alison Palmer (Wheeler), Liz Collins (Watson), Jeni Waterfield, Eileen McGregor (Bond)** and **Jenifer Davidson (Moir).**
Let's hope that this year's reunion in London is not cancelled.

Section 36 (1966)
Section Representative:
Julia Braggins (Cock)

It has been lovely to hear from so many of you again: thank you for making my job so easy and interesting.

Moira Beveridge (Adamson) Ghastly two years (understatement!) as moved four times. Tried flat in London which lasted nine weeks and although fifteen minutes from Sloane Square I hated it - been away too long. Back to Somerset and sort of sofa surfed (very unsettling) and moved into a flat in a retirement block four weeks ago. Very small but I think it will suit as there's really only me, and it means there are people around who notice me if I've sunk without trace! Have decluttered massively and don't miss anything really. Cooking off as I just buy in, as and when. Went on a cruise for seven weeks: India, Sri Lanka, UAE, Bangkok, Malaysia, Hong Kong amongst other places. Quite daunting as not easy on one's own. I shall try again but with more single travellers and no kids! Giving most things a swerve until more me, and no more of the parasites who have been cluttering my life up for last 40 years - shall be on my own (assuming the cash survives!) No WBs around and am becoming a bit of a hermit. Shall try and come to the jamboree in May. Have a bit of polymyalgia which is a bore: caused by too many wet days hunting on Exmoor for twenty-three seasons.

Julia Braggins (Cock) All well in rural Kent. Met up with, and heard from, several WBs this year, which was lovely. Finally met **Jenny Webb** for a coffee, since we live so close. She and I did not coincide at WB at all, it turns out, she being a good few years behind our year, but it was great to meet up and exchange memories! **Jo Clarke (Brooke)** has moved from Devon to Kent, to be closer to her family, and it has been so good to be in touch again. Also, a lovely meeting with **Judy Turner (Marryat)** and **Sandy Marshall (Hellawell)** in a National Trust place which turned out to be a whole lot further away than Sandy and I had reckoned – and we had foolishly chosen a half term week, so the place was heaving. So poor Judy had to spin out her chilli con carne in the café for quite a time while she waited for us, bagging our seats. Am also in touch with **Ronny Boswell**, still living in Florida, and grieving the death of two of her sisters, Angela and Caroline, both of whom died last year. All children and grandchildren flourish (give or take the usual life events) and Peter and I are both well and happy. So, we feel blessed.

Louise Bruce (Stericker) I never think my news is exciting at all. Having retired four years ago to look after our first grandchild (she is now 5) and subsequently her brother, now 3, I am still waiting for my hubby to retire (we have just celebrated our 47th wedding anniversary) so that we can do more things together. Having said that, we have done some wonderful trips in recent years, for example to the Galapagos and also the Arctic Circle – all great fun. Life, however, is not dull as our elder daughter with the two children lives nearby and our younger daughter, who has a progressive, degenerative ataxia, does not drive, and thus I am constantly on the road taking her to hospital appointments etc. We did actually take her on a trip of a lifetime (for her) on the Rocky Mountaineer and a cruise up the inside passage to go whale watching in Alaska last year. As she is more or less wheelchair bound, we came back exhausted, but it is all about making memories for her.

Sarah Ferguson Studland was quiet after the breakdown of the Sandbanks Ferry last summer and we enjoyed the respite from endless speeding traffic. I was delighted to welcome eighteen of our year to the Big 70th Birthday Reunion at Studland Bay House in October. We were blessed with great food and drink offerings and sunshine for our walks and outings. Some came for the three nights, others for less or even just to join in for the day. In November I spent two weeks in Goa with my yoga teacher (Joey Miles from Leeds) and three winter months in Wanaka, New Zealand, enjoying their summer paddle boarding and mountain biking. Retirement certainly suits me, and I am planning to do some ski touring in the Alps and in Crete in April.

Lucy Fisher (Sadleir) 2019 was a very good year. We went to Menorca for two weeks in May and I visited my son, Tim, and family in Sweden in February, August and October. In June we had Tim's 40th celebrations with three other friends hosting which was a five-day extravaganza for about a hundred in Devon so another wonderful family get-together.

In October, **Sarah Ferguson**, (Fergie) organised a wonderful four-day get-together in Studland for fifteen or more of our year to celebrate our 70th birthdays. Such fun! All under one luxurious roof and wonderful reminiscing, walking, and eating and drinking. We had a good Dorchester reunion - **Fergie, Jeni Whittaker (Waterfield), Sooty, myself** and **Liz Watson (now Collins)** who none of us had seen for about fifty years! Brilliant!

I've just celebrated my 70th with all the family and close friends and been spoilt rotten for three days. Roll on 2020!

Veronique Lewis (Hall) Still here although I don't have much in the way of news! We had a wonderful party for family and friends in October. Our daughter, her husband, and our grandson, now 7, came over from Canada for three weeks, to join our son, his wife, our granddaughter (12) and grandson (10), so and it was great having all the family together again. We hadn't seen the Canadians for three years as my husband's mobility problems prevent him from travelling very far.

I am church warden for our village church and as we have no secretary or treasurer on the PCC, guess who has to do it all! It takes up rather more of my time than I envisaged.

It was lovely to hear from **Chris McLaren** with the news of the reunion. Sadly, I won't be able to get to London for the one this year.

Alexandra Marshall (Hellawell) We started this year with flu – a strain that the jab obviously didn't recognise. Working back through what was otherwise a fairly healthy year (though I did break my collar bone when a pavement cyclist shot across a side road and knocked me off my own bike), we got ourselves to Spain and even on to several trains to explore Cordoba and Cadiz.

Back home we explored parts of Lancashire that we've usually driven past on the way to somewhere else: the Forest of Bowland was a revelation. We had another week on Arran with the family, but need to go again, as after two visits we still haven't quite got to the top of Goat Fell.

Another meet-up with Jules and **Judy Turner** at The Vyne, in Hampshire, was a highlight, though these days getting anywhere seems to take so much longer than it used to. On one of the last hot September days, we met up with the family at the Arboretum. All very different of course from the 1960s, but on a walk round we came to a spot near the Silk Wood that was instantly recognisable: I was back in 1965, in grey mac and wellingtons and the white sweater - as close as we got to leisure wear?

Karen Olsen In April 2019 I spent a lovely weekend with **Judy Chesterman** to celebrate her special birthday. We had a splendid lunch at a private room in the London Wetland Centre in Barnes with family and friends. It was a great opportunity to catch up with everyone including **Eileen McGregor (Bond)** and husband Gerald who were also invited.

In May I headed for London again to meet up with **Christine Dayananda (Dias)** and her husband Mahen, who were over here from Sri Lanka. We got together with **Sue Passfield (Ross)** and **Venessa Pugh** for dinner. I went via the Royal Academy where my niece Elana, daughter of my sister **Jackie Woodgate (Olsen)**, is an exhibition manager. I had the chance to catch a couple of exhibitions, then we travelled together so that Elana could join us for a pre-dinner drink. She was keen to see Christine and Mahen too, as she had stayed with them in Sri Lanka a few years ago.

I am looking forward to a reunion of our year from Sections 36 and 37 planned for June 2020 at the London home of **Sultana Al-Quaiti (Rashid).** Hoping to get to Westonbirt on Saturday 16th May to celebrate the 90th anniversary of Westonbirt Association. There appears to be a lot of interest with year groups trying to make up tables for lunch.

Alison Palmer (Wheeler) I can't remember if I replied last year. Anyway, sadly my husband, Mick, of nearly fifty years, died in October 2018. Very unexpected and sudden. We were in the middle of building a house for us to downsize into as an extension to our timber framed house. I finished the building and have now moved into the house which is perfect. It has all been traumatic, but I am getting on with life and adjusting.

I went to our year's get together in Studland hosted by **Sarah Ferguson** in October which was great fun. Good to see old friends. Grandchildren are growing up and range from 16 down to 10, and I am going to be a grandmother again in July, which is exciting.

Alison Parry (Sturdy Morton) Most of my travel this year has been to see children and grandchildren in the USA and France. However, I did get to be one of five sailing a catamaran from Martinique to St Vincent. Sadly, this was the last of several years of Caribbean island sailing, as my dear friend and trusted skipper on these trips died in October.

I spent two weeks in January visiting Ethiopia. The Lalibela rock churches have been on my to-visit list since I was in primary school! They are just as amazing as I had expected. I was in awe. Ethiopia is one of the most Christian countries in the world and also one of the poorest. It has incredibly beautiful and varied countryside where agricultural living is still positively biblical, as though time has stood still. They are charming, very religious, with two non-meat, non-dairy days each week, daily celebrations for the saints and a general use of the ancient orthodox calendar.

Loved our reunion in October, a huge thank you to **Alison Boxley** for organising us and to **Sarah Ferguson** for hosting us. We had pretty amazing weather with sunshine and enjoyed a fabulous few days catching up and exploring the Jurassic coast, while visiting the fossil museum, walking, talking, and eating and drinking exceptionally well!

I continue to enjoy silversmithing, London's various theatres and concert venues, and life in the Barbican.

Tilly Roberts de Zagal (Roberts) 2019-2020 has been a lovely time and a horrible time. Lovely with fun moments accompanied by friends or family. A great example of happy times would be a luxury week with three friends to Termas de Jahuel, just north of Santiago. Warm thermal swimming pools, hot thermal showers, three delicious gourmet meals a day, pisco sours served by an open fire whilst making a jigsaw puzzle etc. The hotel staff helped finish the puzzle in their free time.

The horrible time, here in Chile, has been since October 16th 2019. Metro stations wrecked, supermarkets ransacked and set on fire, graffiti everywhere, streets barricaded, churches set on fire, public transport systems ruined etc. Right now, it's February 2020, the height of the summer holidays, Congress is unwisely taking a break, and things look very bleak for March when businesses start up again. Will very necessary laws have been passed to improve pensions, public education, reduce parliamentarians' exorbitant salaries etc? Highly unlikely, as far as I can see.

In April we are to vote as to whether we want a new constitution. The present one was concocted in the 1980s by Pinochet with no public/parliament input. It's so sad to see a president and a Congress that never saw the people's unrest and have shown themselves to be so inept about solving it.

On a lighter note, the family are all well, and I will be over in the UK in May for a Scottish train trip with three close friends from Froebel (Roehampton University) days. We're still known as 'The Tower Flowers'!

Judy Turner (Marryat) I may be terribly busy but nothing exactly exciting, or, I feel, even interesting to other people.

I have just been to **Sue-Anne Milln**'s funeral, a very full congregation in the church where she used to play the organ. Very sad, far too young.

Meanwhile, despite having Parkinson's, I am still playing tennis, working my two Labradors, gardening, though not much in this weather, and delighting in the fact I have learnt bridge and can play that while the rain is pouring down outside. I am chairman of the Fernhurst Society, which actually is quite fun, but takes up a lot of time. We are about to organise a major litter clear-up round the parish. This is something we do twice a year, and every time we are disgusted by the amount of rubbish we find.

Section 35 (1965)
Section Representative:
Marilyn Jones (Bird)

Diane Charnell I'm still enjoying reasonably good health and keeping busy. I volunteer at my local National Trust property, The Vyne, as a gardener one day a week. I can get involved in anything from edging the lawns to pruning apple trees and clipping hedges. Privately, I also offer my gardening services to elderly and disabled people who wish to remain living in their own homes but have become unable to manage their garden.

I am still a member of Hook Choral Society. Last autumn we were privileged to be conducted by Bob Chilcott in a performance of his recently composed work, Christmas Oratorio. We also regularly perform works by Howard Goodall, whom we are honoured to have as the choral society's Patron. Last October I went on a singing holiday to Venice, joining up with singers from all over the UK and Europe, to rehearse a number of short choral works prior to performing them in a concert in the San Troviso Church.

For the last eight years I have volunteered as a driver for a charity which provides assistance with transport for those in need, principally to medical appointments or shopping. I have also acted as a trustee and secretary for the charity, but have now resigned in order to spend a little less time on my computer and have more opportunity to do more long-haul travel.

In fact, I went to Southern India in January this year with a tour company specialising in holidays for mature single travellers. It was a fantastic experience lasting eighteen days, travelling through three states, including Kerala, and the bonus was missing some horrible weather in the UK!

I am also very much involved with my four grandchildren, now ranging in age from 6 to 19, who live nearby. They all go to different schools or college, so I often have school-run duties.

I am planning to go to the 90th anniversary lunch at Westonbirt on 16th May so hope to catch up with any of my school contemporaries then.

Sian King (Davis) I am continuing to try different sorts of voluntary work here in South Wales. As well as nearing completion of my PhD, I am assisting at Newport Museum and Art Gallery twice a week. This involves a wide range of backroom jobs including cataloguing old photos and helping to set up exhibitions. I am also working for the Newport Medieval Ship, a charity which is conserving and reassembling a large fifteenth-century vessel found in the mud of the River Usk. My contribution is to catalogue and maintain a library of research material. I have also become a trustee of another charity whose mission is to build a community hub in our Monmouthshire village. My intention with all of this (and I haven't mentioned everything!) is to keep as busy as possible although there is still plenty of time for reading and for various family activities.

Marilyn Jones As for myself, we are still spending much time travelling, cruising, and having fun. Just returned from three weeks in Laos – a very interesting country to visit. Eagerly awaiting the arrival of our ninth grandchild, so life is always busy, but very pleasantly so!

Section 34 (1964)
Section Representative:
Julia Popham (Bishop)

Ann Beattie (Buckland) Ann writes to say that she doesn't have anything exciting to report and comments on the extraordinary times we are living in at the moment. She wonders, as I am sure we all do, as to how things are going to progress over the next few months.

Clare Carter (Binney) So, sitting here contemplating a fairly abrupt change from weeks filled with U3A activities to a more contemplative life.

Most of our indoor activities have been cancelled from tomorrow, so no ukulele, cinema, photography and so on. Most weekdays have something of interest, but we are still walking. The U3A is such a great organisation, I've made so many new friends.

My sadness at the moment is that, at the end of March, both children and families were coming for a little while and that is obviously off. Schools are shut in Japan, and Denmark has closed its borders. Luckily, Tomoyo, Kristian and Helen are all able to work from home. It would have been the first time Azuma, now 7, and Finn, 17 months, would have met. We're just hoping to be able to get together later in the year.

Otherwise I visited Denmark in the summer, which was a lovely change of scene, and I also had a very pleasant, but wet, week in Donegal with Jane and Simon. We were in a very remote cottage with an open fire and no wi-fi, and it was lovely to have a bit of quiet time together. Now just wishing for the rain and wind to stop so I can do some gardening.

June Cohen (Kefford) This last year has been dominated by the acceleration of my husband's illness and then his death in April, just three days short of our golden wedding. Much suffering for him, huge sadness for us all, and life-changing impact for me. However, throughout it all the lifelines and buoyancy bags of amazing NHS care, the kindness of friends and strangers, and the overwhelming love of my amazing children and their family have all been awesome. Thank you too to all Westonbirt friends who have played a part in that. It was especially good to spend a lovely day with **Carol Brawn (Topham)** and her husband and to reconnect by email with **Sue Coveney (Hyman)** and **Deni Bittolo (Porter)**.

Family trips to Genoa and Tuscany were highlights of the summer as were many other precious times with family and friends. Memories and sadness are all important parts of the journey, but it is amazing, too, how the straightforward exuberance of little people always lifts the spirits! Just recently my two eldest boys have done a fantastic job of refitting my kitchen, and I am now looking forward to a trip to the Holy Land next month and other trips and holidays in the pipeline. I have so very much to be grateful for. I look forward to seeing some 'old' friends at WB in May.

Philippa Dutton (Thomson) I loved my working life, but I am enjoying retirement just as much. In January we cruised with the Assam Bengal Navigation company down the Hugli River in India. A totally fascinating trip on a *Death on the Nile* style, extremely civilised cruise ship, with a friendly crew who could not do too much for us. Each day we were taken to different villages, temples, and sites along the river, and in the evenings we watched films about the history and source of the Ganges. We spent a few days of R and R at the end of the trip in South Goa. March saw me skiing for the first time in twenty-eight years in Lech where the conditions could not have been better. I was shocked to find helmets now compulsory, boots three times as heavy as those I was used to, and the skis were shorter. I managed, met some kindred spirits to ski with, and because the conditions were perfect my non-skiing husband Dickie was able to join us for lunch up the mountain most days.

In May we enjoyed another Bike and Barge holiday, this time up the Rhine and Neckar rivers, cycling along the banks enjoying wine, attractive villages and sites including Heidelberg, with twenty-eight other cyclists, all nationalities.

Visits to Glyndebourne, Garsington and Grange Park opera with friends are the annual summer opera treats and this year our outside picnic was not rained off once – definitely a first for many years. We returned to our favourite Turkish resort Kalkan in September for guaranteed sun, lovely friends we meet there every year, and delicious food.

I was 'clothed' as a Liveryman of the Worshipful Company of Musicians in April and continue to enjoy all the events offered by that splendid company as well as volunteering for their outreach programme, accompanying young talented musicians into deprived primary schools. I am also involved as a Friend of the Musicians Church, which I find most rewarding. Fortunately, I can still sing. Having just taken part in a B Minor Mass performance with the English Chambers Singers, under the baton of Martin Neary, I am also enjoying being a member of The Academy Choir in Wimbledon, conducted by Matthew Best. Rehearsal for both choirs is minimal, being just a couple of weeks or so before the concert. It is very rewarding to sing with talented professionals and good amateurs.

Coronavirus permitting, Dickie and I are off to Canada at the end of May to visit my nephew who has settled there. I am in fairly regular touch with **Eleanor Fountaine (Bateman), Julia Popham (Bishop), Jessamy Reynolds (Smith)** and **Gay Kaye (Vernon).** Jessamy and her husband Michael gave a lovely party for their golden wedding last year, and we are lucky enough to be going to the golden wedding of **Gay** and Colin in April.

Charlotte Essex (Humpidge) Richard and I had a memorable trip to Thailand, visiting the main sites in Bangkok, Ayutthaya, Chiang Mai, the Bridge over the River Kwai, the War Cemetery (a moving experience), and Ratchabari, where our daughter-in-law Gal's parents live. A few days were spent on Ko Samet Island which was very relaxing. At home we have had double glazing fitted in the downstairs windows of the cottage which has made a huge difference, hopefully upstairs might be done next. The garden is far too big, but such a joy. Richard's Probus meetings included a trip to Big Pit in Wales and a narrow boat cruise on the Kennet and Avon canal. Richard is still dealing in antiques part-time and continues to restore old weapons. He's had a number of health issues with numerous hospital visits over the last few months. The tumour very close to the pancreas in the upper abdomen has been removed and then onto radiography for other problems.

My sister, **Sue Bowden (Humpidge)**, and her husband Andrew celebrated a milestone birthday and fifty years plus of blessed life together. It was a wonderful family occasion with many of their old friends. Offspring doing their own thing, two boys in Bristol and daughter in London – lovely seeing them quite often.

Susan Fisher (Barritt) Nothing much to report – still enjoying retirement by the sea and also spending some time at our flat in London, the best of both worlds! At home I am very involved with my local church and trying to keep myself reasonably fit. I sometimes look after my grandson (13) when my daughter, Sarah, goes away for work. Although she is single, she adopted him five years ago and after having problems she learnt a way of parenting based on non-violent resistance. This helped her enormously and now she teaches many other parents and professionals how to use the same method. She has written two books, one about her adoption journey and the other about connective parenting using NVR. I am obviously very proud of the way she has gone from helping one child to recover from trauma to helping hundreds of others.

Susan Fraser (Stanton) I don't have much news, like most people I imagine. My husband Martin has Alzheimer's which is progressing slowly, and we are managing fine for the moment. I am still busy with my textile art and have pieces in five exhibitions in the next six months so that is keeping me busy. I won't be at the WB celebrations in May as that day is our golden wedding anniversary and we are planning to have some sort of celebration, even if it is rather low key. I keep in touch with **Judy Winchester (Brown)** and manage a brief visit occasionally, as our son lives outside Banbury and there is a bus to Oxford.

Claire Marshall Major personal news was the birth of Elora Lynn Elaine Murray on 10th May 2019 – a much awaited delight for her parents – and me! Elora is a contented baby and passing milestones like mad. Travel was therefore limited to trips to Nova Scotia.

Although I thought 2019 would be my last year as Chair of OrKidstra, fate intervened and tragically. Our new Chair was in the position for barely a month before her sudden death. I'm back in the saddle until we find another. Enjoying it as always but with a tinge of regret as you can imagine. Six major choral performances since last March with more planned for March, May June, and July... but that's creeping into next year's news.

Julia Popham (Bishop) Once again I am so very grateful to everybody from our Section who replied this year. It's always great to hear from you and as we all get a bit older it really is all the more important to keep in touch with each other, and especially in the current climate of global uncertainty. We continue to keep busy with various local activities and had a wonderful holiday in Croatia last September. We hope to have a week in Norfolk with our son and his family in May. I am in touch with **Joyce Seaman (Carnegie)**, **Eleanor Fountaine (Bateman)** and **Pippa Dutton (Thomson)** and hope to get to the school celebrations in May.

Christine Schoeb (Bryans) I have been in touch with **Anne Grocock** and **Helen Faircliff,** and hope to attend the Westonbirt celebrations in May, maybe a joint Section 34/35 table.

Joyce Seaman (Carnegie) Life is not boring, far from it, but it is not really newsworthy, particularly considering everything else going on in the world at the moment. Our only major family event is the engagement of our son to a delightful Bulgarian girl who works for an investment bank in New York. He is also in the financial world there, so they frequently just pass as clouds in the night, with their ridiculous work schedules. Their wedding is planned for June in Florence, so we may be having to think again. I continue to work at the Ashmolean Museum, for the Japanese keeper, and we are having a large Tokyo exhibition in the summer to coincide with the Olympics. We hope both will be able to go ahead... uncertain times.

Joanna Wilson (Forcey) The last year has been one of travelling backwards and forwards to South Africa, a week with my brother and his wife and friends in Corfu and a walking holiday in Tuscany, which was amazing.

My son and his wife live in Johannesburg and produced an unexpected third child last February. Both my daughters have lived in London for many years but last year the elder, Tembe, and her husband, bought a country house in Kent, near Benenden, where their three daughters go to school, so most weekends are spent there, with weekdays in London, although she is now converting the old carriage house to a studio for painting and sculpture so I suspect more time will be spent in Kent. My younger daughter Rachel has rented out her flat in Hackney and moved to Kent as well, where they are expecting their first baby in April.

I stay with **Anthea Shipley (Franklin-Adams)** each June when I go down for Grandparents Day at Benenden and on occasion have met **Jessamy Reynolds (Smith)** whose granddaughter is also there. I have also met up with **Eleanor Fountaine (Bateman), Jane Simpson (Witt)** and **Liz Grayley (Constance). June Cohen (Kefford)** and I are hoping to go to the reunion at Westonbirt together in May, but with this pandemic who knows!

Section 33 (1963)
Section Representative:
Helen Faircliff (Wienholt)

Susanne Burroughs (Bradbury) A difficult year with my daughter having six months of chemo and then three of radiotherapy. After that she had a jab which is supposed to stop the cancer going to the bones. This flattened her and made her joints unreliable. But she seems to be OK at the moment. I just keep my fingers crossed.

I had a new hip in June which has been a great success. Had a letter in *The Times* as they had been having correspondence regarding retirement and golf. I wrote in that I was playing croquet again three weeks after the op. which I don't think golfers would have been able to do, plus croquet helps keep the brain functioning!

I am off to Lanzarote to play bridge and enjoy the winter sun. In May I am away with the ramblers and in September I am going to Croatia again.

Sue Coveney (Hyman) We had a wonderful visit to Sudeley Castle and grounds last November. It was worth the drive to enjoy the glorious Gloucestershire autumn sunlight. This was followed by a short December trip to Manhattan to catch up with colleagues and theatre. Hoping to learn a bit more Italian before a Ravenna and Bologna trip which is planned for March.

Have seen **Alannah Rylands (Watson Hall)** who continues to be a brilliant gardener and grandmother, plus visited both her daughters. Also enjoyed seeing **Caroline Henderson (Beloe)**, **Julia Tingle** and **Helen Faircliff**. And enjoy our granddaughters who keep me on my toes.

Anita Dudley (Armstrong) says she has no fresh news this year. However, she says she 'won playing bridge in Istanbul, and has also played in UK, Spanish and Indian tournaments this year. I'm too old to play tennis now. Still waiting to see more of you in Mallorca!'

Helen Faircliff (Wienholt) My main news is that last April I became a granny to Abigail Charlotte Wienholt Faircliff who grows apace and is now 10 months old, and very pleased with herself as she has now found out she can stand unaided.

I spent six weeks in my caravan during June and July in Gascony, southern France, and it was good to meet up with friends made from previous camp, and also **Di Vaughan (Hughes)** joined me for a week staying locally. We did the tourist bit each day and enjoyed chatting and swimming. We were reduced to hysterics wriggling into our swimming costumes when we were so hot. Incredible temperature with one week hitting 42°. So, it was a case of reading under the trees, drinking gallons of water and having a swim in the early evening. Mercifully the temperature plummeted at night, so it was easy to sleep. I resumed my French lessons and did another patisserie course. The time went far too quickly.

During the year I have seen **Suz Burroughs (Bradbury)**, **Sue Coveney (Hyman)**, **Mandy Lyne (Smith)**, **Liz Davies (Edwards)** and **Lin Lingwood (Maiden)** who was over from South Africa.

Mary Gillam (Woodrow) We both keep busy without doing very much of interest to anyone else. I spend time walking our elderly blind dog who still enjoys life, so long may it last. I belong to a book group which is super and also we belong to the Art Society, a retired doctors' lunch club, two garden groups and various village things, all of which keep us entertained.

I have met up with **Gay Woodley** again after 50+ years which is super.

Sandra Russell (Morris) We had three weeks in New Zealand last February visiting family, and I had a nice trip to Iceland with my sister **(Fiona)** in the summer; my third visit! Otherwise we have had lots of guests, the occasional weekend away and life goes on as usual. Still playing bridge, doing lots of gardening and busy with the Arts Society, Fife.

Jane Simpson (Witt) In spite of such a very wet winter we haven't suffered any flooding so far this year which has been a miracle. Having taken on a rescue Golden Retriever from Turkey at the end of May, it certainly has been a nightmare taking her for walks with the endless mud, though. John had a hip replacement in October and has recovered very well but still has a lot of problems with his knees, so that looks to be the next thing.

We have another grandson arriving at the beginning of March. It will be number three for our daughter and husband, so that will be exciting and probably at number seven our last grandchild! John turns eighty in March and the whole family are off to Tresco for a week, which will be wonderful. **Liz Graley (Constance)** and **Jo Wilson (Forcey)** were here for lunch in the summer.

Kate Thompson (Richards) A week or two ago I heard *Ramblings* about people climbing Glastonbury Tor. There used to be a sixth-form retreat, the last event being a walk up to Glastonbury Tor on Sunday afternoon. I wonder if this still happens but somehow doubt it.

We now spend more time in Norfolk. I go to London once a week on a Wednesday for an Italian class, the Art Society and the St Michael's Chorale in which I sing. I recently returned from Barbados - a lovely fortnight in the middle of winter. Last year we visited Calabria, a not much visited region of Italy, and an opera festival in Sicily; various small opera houses originally built for the aristocracy have been restored and they are a wonderful setting for first class music. We also had a good week in a Landmark Trust property in Devon when our granddaughter's choir was singing in Exeter Cathedral. Our grandson 'retired' as a Chorister at Westminster Abbey in July and is now at Gresham's School in Norfolk. Schools do seem to keep their pupils very busy these days.

Section 32 (1962)
Section Representative:
Sarah Rundle (Milner)

Denise Bittolo (Porter) They say no news is good news! Nothing special to tell you this year. We had a terribly hot summer last year and have been told to expect an even worse one this year as our winter has been very, very mild. I plan on escaping to rainy Scotland should it get too much by August! September we will be flying over to Tenerife to see our eldest son and family.

Elizabeth Bryant I've just got back from an extremely wet and muddy walk along the local tow path. The river burst through the flood defences a few nights ago, flooding the local hotel and cellars of various shops. Then the water table overflowed, and water came streaming down my little hill. Everything is very soggy but not nearly as bad as for those poor people in Gloucestershire who have been flooded for the third time this year. What with floods here, horrendous bushfires in Australia, COVID-19 and swarms of locusts, it's positively Biblical.

European travel only this year. I went back to the hotel in Paris to which my godmother had taken me exactly 62 years ago. It had scarcely changed at all, and the manager took me into the dining room to find "our" table. Copenhagen and Brussels again, with friends, and most recently Vienna for the first time, specifically to see the Caravaggio exhibition (disappointing, I thought). In June I'm going to stay in France with a friend I haven't seen for about 50 years. At the moment I'm trying to find a holiday which combines Thessaloniki with a few days doing nothing in the sun.

I am still frequently in touch with **Phil Shaw (Northcroft)** and **Mary Hudson** and continue to enjoy living near Bath.

Mary Hudson No major updates this year, but still soldiering on. Excellent holiday down the Nile last autumn. I have always wanted to see Karnak and the Great Pyramid at Giza - but so it seems did half the world on the same days! Meanwhile still meeting up with a few old WB friends as and when.

Erica Rigg (Harding) This past year has been a generally happy one, despite the sadness of several more friends and relatives dying. My replacement hip is still marvellous, and activities I thought I'd had to give up through old age are possible again: climbing hills, carrying small children on my back, walking and running reasonable distances without pain, using the gym several times a week, etc. (Clearly my body is not as worn out as I had thought!)

We have five grandchildren, and the oldest has now left school to train as a deck officer at the Nautical College. At present he is on a ship being tossed around on a stormy North Sea as part of the practical content. He's coped so far, although it sounds pretty hard work, so I hope he continues to see it as an adventure. He's all set to be the youngest captain ever of course...! The others are all at school, some nearing public exams and the others enjoying primary school still. Luckily, I see all of them quite frequently as three live nearby in Glasgow, and the others in Saltaire, near Bradford, which is quite accessible to us.

I was thinking about Westonbirt recently and wondering yet again why cloaks were abandoned as part of the uniform. They were so comfortable and easy to slip on when going between buildings. In fact, my first introduction to WB was as 'the school that wore cloaks'. Could anyone enlighten me about this? I'd be really interested to know. Thanks.

Sarah Rundle (Milner) Firstly, thank you so much to everyone who has replied to my pleas for News – I am extremely grateful.

How my life has changed since Robin died. I am still in the same house, same friends, etc, but miss him so much. I am lucky in that I have a wonderful family who keep me going as well as my two Golden Retrievers, especially the ten year old, who still jumps up onto a seat Robin would sit on when out for a walk on the coastal path. She then looks at me as if to say, 'where is he?'

I had a most enjoyable holiday in Scotland in July. Claire, eldest daughter, and grandson, Sam, joined me and then in October I spent a lovely week in Wales with our son, Jon, and his family.

I am still singing in a local choir – very involved in that as I am librarian, which is a thankless task!

I continue to thank Westonbirt for teaching me to sing properly and for my love of classical music. Caerhays Castle Gardens keep me busy in the spring and trying to sort out church matters during an interregnum also keeps me occupied and somewhat frustrated!

As Claire lives near Bristol, I have started to visit the Westonbirt Arboretum fairly regularly which we, and our dogs, thoroughly enjoy. We also spent a wonderful day, just down the road, at Highgrove, in August.

How I echo all **Sue Whitfield** has said over Brexit. Our daughter, Nicola, and family, who live in Toulouse, are finding it all very hard. So many British people have applied for French nationality, it is taking a long time for their applications to be processed. Nicola teaches in a university in Toulouse and is extremely concerned for her Erasmus students. I am concerned for the future of all our grandchildren.

I am hoping to meet up with **Sue Whitfield** and **Deb Soper** later in the year and keep in touch with **Elizabeth Bryant**.

Lynda Scott Williams After a somewhat peripatetic lifestyle, I've just clocked up five great years here in vibrant Bridport, West Dorset. I'm very active within U3A, which took me to Cirencester last year. Whilst there I took the opportunity to drive through WB. My first visit since 1963! I was amazed to see just how many cars were parked there. Students as well as staff, I guess.

I'm also busy keeping up with far-flung and travelling family. Sadly, my own travelling days have to be behind me, but they all make up for it. My stepdaughter is living and working in Dubai, while my stepson's job (working for a risk management company that deals with flood, fire and pestilence!) takes him to all cities between Singapore and Silicon Valley, Montreal and Monte Carlo. My nieces and nephew travel extensively too. One niece has been living in Valencia and Porto, working for a charity that focuses on delivering practical outcomes, such as building a hospital and training midwives in Syria. She is now looking at moving to South America.

Apart from my much-missed friend **Rosemary Loverock**, I've not been in touch with any of my WB contemporaries, but I am in touch with my old drama college friends.

This year I had to resign from chairing my local branch of the brilliant charity, Remap, who do fantastic work nationally for people with disabilities. Do look them up - they might be able to help you and yours. Or perhaps you could help them?

Deborah Soper I now have a busier weekly schedule than for some time, mostly revolving round a couple of community art groups, one of which is a drop-in session, the other occasional themed courses which run for eight weeks at a time. They have turned around my own artwork by getting me over a block I'd had since my last exhibition in 2015. In between, in the fallow period, I have been attending quite a lot of life drawing and a pottery groups, which still continue, and they are all great fun and have made me more productive. If I can, I attend other occasional courses when they happen, such as lino printing. It all makes me wonder why I read zoology at Oxford instead of going to art school! But it has all worked out well as it is.

I saw quite a lot of my younger son in the first part of last year: he broke his leg skating (for the first time) with his daughter, and it didn't heal first time around, and his flat was impossible on crutches, so you can imagine the rest! We went to visit Grace in Shrewsbury in February and he could still walk twice as fast as me on his crutches!

The American contingent of my family, my sister's daughter and grandchildren, came over for a multiple celebration of 50th and 21st birthdays and a 25th wedding anniversary in June, so I took the ferry and my car over and much enjoyed all the catching up.

I took the opportunity to visit Grace again and caught up with **Sue Whitfield (Bottomley)** and **Carolyn Halliday (Wheeler)**. The latter was a sad occasion because it was the memorial service of her husband Tim, who used to be a prof at the Open University and was also a talented artist. It was a good occasion with a humanist celebration in New College Chapel. I returned the next day to take the opportunity to actually talk to Carolyn who still lives in a four-story north Oxford house. Incidentally, her three children all have PhDs!

In the summer, Grace came to visit us for a holiday, which was very exciting, and I am happy to say she is coming back this year, so we are looking forward to that very much.

After my return from the UK, I have been hanging about in a sense, waiting for my hip replacement, which finally happened on December 19th. So, Christmas lunch was cottage pie! My sister brilliantly came and saw me through the first three weeks. It is now six weeks and it has all gone very well. I am ready to plan a trip over to the UK towards the end of April (when I should have recovered from my forthcoming cataract op). Like many others, I dare say, I am beginning to feel like a bionic woman. If anyone who remembers me is coming over to Guernsey, do get in touch.

Sue Whitfield (Bottomley) The years roll by, and as the grandchildren get older each year, so do the rest of us! We have remained stable at eleven since last year, ranging from one taking GCSEs this summer to another hitting aged two at the same time. Our son and daughter-in-law recently told us that their children (who will be aged 4 and 2) are due to enter reception and nursery at Westonbirt Prep next academic year – they live and work quite near the school. They will be the third generation on site – my mother went to Westonbirt soon after the school opened, followed by my sister **Jane** and myself in the 50s and 60s. After a generational break, these two will be in the building we knew as the San, where I lived for a couple of weeks after having my appendix out when there was a bit of a cluster of cases in about 1958. They serve better food now! I'm sure my little grandchildren will love it there. My other children and their families also bowl along merrily, and we see them when we can, either here in Gloucestershire or where they variously live.

As well as being granny, I have taken up art exhibitions with a vengeance, having never, until retirement, really had a chance to learn anything about art. Now it is becoming a bit of an addiction as the more one gets to see and learn, the more eager one becomes.

Last year, the stand-out exhibition I went to was of the paintings by Sorolla at the National Gallery. I went three times, absolutely stunned by his depiction of light, and his brilliance in the tender portraits of his family and others, and the gardens, landscapes, social and political conscience shockers, and seaside life with children and boats. It may not sound exciting, but I do recommend everyone to go if they are ever near the paintings in Spain or anywhere else. I do not know why we have not seen more of them in the UK before; everyone I recommended it to, who went, was thrilled by it – artists and beginners alike – and almost no-one had heard of him before, yet in his time he was world-renowned elsewhere.

It was a pleasure to have lunch with **Deb Soper** again this year while she was visiting her sister in Cirencester, and it is always enjoyable, too, to hear from **Sarah** when she so kindly nudges us into contributing to the magazine, and then reading about others.

I am trying to accept the loss of EU membership but am finding that, and the accompanying changes which are rolling in, very hard. It is definitely time to concentrate on sowing the seeds for summer vegetables, and in this time (as I write) of appalling floods, being grateful about living at the top of a hill. Meanwhile our descendants who are settled in France are taking up French citizenship. And so the generations roll, along with the years.

Gay Woodley (Durston) I have had a good year. First grandchild taking GCSEs, she seemed to work extremely hard with great dedication. I don't remember doing anything like the work she did with masses of revision (though I do recall revising under the bedclothes at the last minute).We had a couple of nights at Bovey Castle, being very spoiled, and then three good fun days with the family in Bude so the children could learn to surf; Cornwall was gorgeous, Devon was foggy! My daughter has developed a new Airbnb in her garden in the Black Mountains, The Bothy in the Clouds, which is fantastic - views and breakfast to die for! We now have to book in to go and stay.

We went on a cruise around Sicily in October, which was so interesting. **Helen Bianchi** came to Rutland on a sunny day in July and we had lunch in the garden of Hambleton Hall followed by a lovely evening in the garden and beautiful, award winning theatre, at the Nevill Holt Opera. I enjoyed going to a sing-along there in the autumn. Opera class continues, *Death in Venice* this term. We went to Aldeburgh in September, to a wonderful concert at Snape Maltings, with Nicola Benedetti, and then the *Symphony Fantastique*, both performed later at the proms.

Because of a few problems in our Arts Society, I have become Chairman again, after twenty years! It's quite a lot of work, as half the Committee are completely new and need their hands holding, and the way things are done now are somewhat different to the 1990s. You never can get away with the emails coming fast and furious.

Yoga and a dance class keep me on the move as well as walking my twelve-year-old terrier, who is getting a bit slow now.

Good wishes to everyone.

Section 31 (1961)
Section Representative:
Priscilla Llewelyn (Rickard)

Thank you all so, so much for your news and comments regarding our section.

Sadly, but inevitably, members get less year by year, but in a way I hope that makes it even more worthwhile to read about each other - it has been great to hear from some people who were roused into indignation when asked if they were still alive. Thank you so much to everyone for keeping the Section going in such a very interesting way.

If anyone would like to be put in touch with another member, I can send your request to them directly, for them to contact you.

Since starting to write this, the Big C Virus has hit us all, wherever we live. Joins us up worldwide in an odd sort of way. I do hope we all stay well, and, if it gets us, that it's not too unpleasant or indeed life threatening. Best wishes to everyone. P.

Vanessa Cook (Hall) From North Yorkshire. Still alive! Still running the garden and plant nursery and feeding visitors with delicious cakes. Have nine grandchildren and two great-grandchildren. Two new knees and two new hips - the wonderful NHS keeps me rushing around when so many friends are not so lucky.

Jane Drew (Mason) From Bristol. Yes, I'm alive! I am not in touch any more with anyone from Westonbirt, although always look at news and information from the emails as I have occasionally visited the school for various functions.

I now have two grandchildren, girls aged 3 and 1. The three-year-old lives just around the corner so I see her a lot, which is lovely. Otherwise, I continue my hobbies of art, bridge, gardening, and holidays. I have recently had a terrible cough lasting two months so am fearful of COVID-19 coming this way!

Wendy Earl (Lloyd-Kirk) From Cornwall. I'm still alive but slowing up noticeably! However, I'm still much involved with local affairs - doing some church work as a licensed lay minister, chairman of the Friends of Menacuddle Well (historic riverside garden with holy well) and Future Proofing (climate emergency group).

Last summer I met with **Jane Kopsch (Capleton)**, **Jane Pilgrim (Begg)** and **Patmalar Thuraisingham**. We had such a super day at WB and were able to go all over the house as the kids weren't there, and all in glorious sunshine.

Rosie Edgington (Heygate) From Norfolk. This is just to say yes I am still alive. But what strange scary times we are living in and not great to be over 70. I live by myself with my dog in the middle of nowhere by the sea so I can at least go for good walks. My children are the ones who tell me I must keep away from everyone and actually I think they are probably right - I know we are the elderly but I don't want to die just yet although I do understand 'survival of the fittest' is a possible but rather un-PC statement! So, I have said no to a bridge invitation on Thursday and various other social events.

Sue Harrison From Bath. I retired from the Metropolitan Police civil staff in 1998 after thirty years, and then worked part-time for City University in London for 10 years – a good way to make the change to full-time retirement. Since then I have spent my time at home in Bath or in the flat in London, keeping up with family, friends and social activities in both areas. I'm still involved in family history research, hosting a U3A group in Bath and acting as Bath treasurer for the Bristol and Avon FHS society. The London societies seem to concentrate on wine tasting, although I do organise pétanque for one French group and act as secretary for another.

As far as holidays are concerned, I have given up long holidays abroad, mainly concentrating on short river cruises in Europe at the moment. I haven't been back to Westonbirt for some years despite it being relatively close. I do keep in contact with **Fiona Crosthwaite Eyre (Hunter Russell)** from our section and we met up in London recently.

Jane Kopsch (Capleton) From Bristol. I am still alive!

Priscilla Llewelyn (Rickard) From Monmouthshire. I've been quite busy again this year, moving up the road into my own house after three years spent renovating it.

Life in retirement is proving ok. I have returned to writing stories for the grandchildren (usually appreciated more by their parents at present, but I live in hope). I recommend this as a therapeutic pastime, although you all seem so busy that this may fall on deaf ears. Otherwise life passes as expected when getting older, but certainly with some compensations. I'm lucky enough to have nine lovely grandchildren, and I now find that a much more carefree do-as-you-please way of life also seems quite possible. When I think back to my own grandmothers and their stodgy lives, I feel very fortunate!

Jane Merritt (Wilkinson) From North Carolina USA. It has been another busy year with church activities and prison ministry. Keith and I are still very active preaching weekly at one prison and visiting another a couple of times a week. We have a capital campaign currently to upgrade our nave, and to build a new pipe organ to replace the existing one. I am on a Spiritual Emphasis sub-committee to encourage evangelism as we seek to renew the physical and spiritual wellbeing of our church members.

We visited Michael and the grandchildren in Copenhagen again last summer. We helped them downsize from their villa to an apartment in a delightful suburb of Copenhagen (Charlottenlund). Cecilia and Marcus (22 and 20) are both studying at the University of Copenhagen's School of Business. They went to Australia for three weeks before Christmas and are all skiing in Austria as I write this. I still enjoy working out at the gym a few times a week, and I go for a four-mile jog most mornings. We are blessed with good health and a very fulfilling life. I wish I could participate in the 90th birthday activities. I shall be thinking of you all and wish you much enjoyment.

Patricia Mounsey (Bennion) From Wiltshire. I don't really have much news. My second husband, Simon, died in December 2018, John Irwin (first husband) having died in 1993, so that's not very good news unfortunately. I live in a house Simon and I built in 2005, and he created an amazing garden out of the agricultural field we built the house in, and I spend a lot of my time in it. I have hens and did have bantams, but the fox got them. Don't know what else to write, all pretty mundane stuff. My cottage is on the market with Blount and Maslin of Malmesbury, but unofficially until the market picks up.

Meg Paige (Fleury) From Bath. We are both still very much alive and very well as I write. Nick turned 80 in the summer just after we celebrated our

55th wedding anniversary. Also in the summer, the second of our ten grandchildren was married, and he and his wife are expecting a daughter this summer. Where did the time go? All our children live near us and we have been involved in theirs and their families lives which has been wonderful. They are all such a joy.

We still enjoy travelling, although it's not so environmentally friendly, so we're limiting ourselves now. But we do have a trip to Canada this summer to meet family. That sounds so ordinary but it's not. I did a DNA test last year and discovered that I am 57% French and in fact Acadian. I did this as I was an adopted child after the war, and although I searched for and found my mother and five half siblings, I was unable to find my father, who she said was Canadian. Canada has strict privacy, but the DNA threw up all my relatives. After much research, I discovered my father, who had died, but his children are alive, so I have four more siblings. I contacted them and we are all looking forward to getting to know each other. I am the eldest of ten, three mothers and one father. So, Canada is an exciting trip to close the loop of a long search of discovery that tells me who I am and where I come from.

Sue Patchett (Greenwood) From Sydney, Australia. I'm alive. No news - just fires and flooding rains. We only had to put up with the smoke smell and ashes during the fires – not nice. Flooding rains gratefully received - our new Prime minister not so much. We sold our farm at Wallabadah five years ago.

I have a chronic cough and as you can imagine, I can clear a room in a second! I believe you have run out of loo paper too - people are mad.

Gillian Wynes (Ross Goobey) From Somerset. I spent two weeks in Southmead Hospital, Bristol, in September, with sepsis, but you don't want to hear any more about that. Life jogs on at the 'Independent Living with Care' building which I live in. This means it is independent living, and care if you need it, which I hope will not be any time soon. We have a weekly film show, and a speaker once a month on all sorts of topics. We also have quiz nights and classical music nights.

Section 30 (1960)
Section Representative:
Jane Reid (Bottomley)

Sadly, **Carolyn Reynolds (Mathison)** died in May 2019 from septicemia following a heart valve operation for critical aortic stenosis. Her daughter had put her own contact address in an automatic response for messages (such as the January 2020 mailing) sent to Carolyn, and explained the situation when I got in touch.

Emails to **Sue Trevani (Steer)** bounced – I would appreciate her current email address.

Ann Beard (Harverson), Penelope Cowell (Bowring), Jill McEwan (Montgomerie), Joan Madonko (Scott), Jane Palestrini (Drew), Anne Rennie (McCullagh) and **Sallie Sullivan (Sanderson)** have been in contact during the year.

Jennifer Greatwood (Bawtree) has acknowledged mailings.

Bodhiniya (Ann Udal) had moved, just over a year ago, into her current flat, which might well be her last home, unless she goes into a nursing home, one never knows! She was pleased with the move. She had to do a complete redecoration, carpets, curtains etc, and, of course, some bits of new furniture - things never quite fit the same in a different shaped space. So that took energy last year. She is well placed, at easy walking distance to two of her daughters, shops, two good parks, and the Buddhist Centre she is involved with (in an old house opposite the church her son got married in). The church bells ring - badly - on Sunday mornings and Tuesday evenings. A man in another flat went and talked to the vicar about silencing the bells, unsuccessfully. Bodhiniya enjoys them, despite the bell ringers' poor timing. She has discovered that her mother was born in the end house of the road, so she hasn't gone far.

On the health front, she is pretty well, apart from slightly strange eye symptoms, including a few episodes of double vision, so she has given up driving, as the double vision came on without warning, at random, although only for about five minutes each time. The diagnosis remains unknown, although 'nasties' have been ruled out through a day at the eye hospital, and a day in an emergency stroke clinic, including an MRI scan. She is not missing the car as much as she had expected, partly because she is five minutes' walk from the 'busiest bus route in Europe', which takes her to the start of most places she wants to go to. She feels fortunate that she is not in any pain.

On the whole, she has been feeling fairly reflective over the last few months. She was pleased to spend time with her family, watch her grandchildren grow up, and help out where she could. She does very little teaching at the Buddhist Centre now, although she sees quite a few people. She volunteered in a project for homeless and vulnerable people. Although it could be challenging, she was often amazed by how kind and polite clients were, despite their sometimes appalling difficulties.

She will not be at the May anniversary but sends lots of love to those that do go. She looks forward to reading people's news.

Phoebe Field (Northcroft)'s year slid by, with good visits from family earlier in the year. Their daughter's family near Mount Cook gave them reason to go south to see them or meet halfway in Christchurch. It was fun to see the next generation grow. Family tree research still took up time inside, when too hot or cold or wet or dry. **Maggie (Hughes,** Section 31**)** would not be coming to New Zealand on her annual trip anymore, and Pat (Weaver) (not an Association member) was moving closer to Nelson.

Lesley Godwin (Neill) emailed that after the excitement of 2018, when she had the trip of a lifetime to Australia (travelling on the Ghan train from Adelaide to Darwin), meeting up with **Anne McCullagh** (now **Rennie** and a very successful writer - thank you **Warb**?!) for a marvellous afternoon together when the years melted away (Anne was one of Lesley's bridesmaids in 1968), before then visiting Bali and Singapore, 2019 was quieter. She lives in the same little house they bought in 1972 in a delightful part of Vancouver in British Columbia, Canada. She feels blessed with a daughter and family who only live twenty minutes away - her two grandsons (9 and 11) were a total joy and played just about every sport under the sun (except lacrosse – ahh! - horrid memories). The older one sails at the Royal Vancouver Yacht club, and there couldn't be a more glorious location for it - sea, mountains, city high rises in the distance. Her son lives on Vancouver Island, happily busy with the Naval reserve - no additional family yet.

Christ Church Cathedral is important in Lesley's life, as are her friends, her garden, choral music (does anyone remember singing the Haydn *Creation* with Monkton Combe? Lesley was a soloist (thanks **Winnie Law**!) and was so petrified that she froze, and good old **Anne** took over for her!, and always poetry. Lesley's last beloved cat Kit died 4 years ago, and she cannot bear to replace her to have her heart broken again.

She ended 'Life changes with all our friends and loved ones as we creak on. And what a world we live in! *Bono malum superate* - as I always say as my annual amaryllis comes through the door, but always gratitude for those years at WB; Canon **Howard**, **EAMC**, and gratitude for learning those evening hymns which we sang at Vespers, always with me into my decrepitude. Gratitude for WB! Lucky us. Love to all.'

Janet Kingston (Oakeley) emailed that going to Melbourne earlier this year meant that their visit coincided with the Australian Tennis Championships, red dust from the horrendous bush fires and temperatures up to 43°C. As always, it was good to see their eldest daughter who, though busy at work, did manage to find time to take them out and about and enabled Janet to see some of her favourite places once more. She commented that even though she has gained more replacement parts, she managed to keep going and enjoy her visits back to WB - even to supporting her youngest daughter who participated in regular races through the grounds as and when her Major duties permitted. Their middle daughter is still running marathons, so guess who has to look after the family? Janet hopes to catch up again with old girls in the summer (if it goes ahead).

Carol Mullin (Rostron) said that it might be possible to get to the gathering on 16th May, and that sixty years since leaving school was a serious anniversary!

Roma Part (Thorpe) was widowed in December 2019, so her learning curve did another vertical take-off. She hoped that 2020 would see her join the e-world, but her occupation when she wrote was trying to empty clothes from the garage. Roma has also included some special memories, which appear elsewhere in this magazine. (*(Editor's note: These special memories will now be included in the material we will put together next year, as part of the delayed celebration of the Association's 90th anniversary).*

Juliet Peel (de Galleani) had good news about **Elizabeth Hawken (Avens)** with whom she had had a lovely lunch. Elizabeth was on excellent form, having made a very good recovery from her stroke some years ago with just some left-sided problems remaining. She drove and was independent, still showing the steely determination she had always had! She took an opportunity to coach Juliet's husband to try to get him to walk properly! (She was a physio!)

Jane Reid (Bottomley) finally trailed off the drugs for GCA at the end of 2019 but she has not yet become organized enough to regain some fitness. Walking fast does not seem to be a sensible option after tripping in the street, smashing glasses, and having to have stitches in the muscles as well as the skin of her forehead. Her younger grandchild hoped that there would be a Harry Potter scar – 'the Granny who lived' – but the surgeon said it would take six months for a scar to stabilize into its final form.

Rosemary Somers (Fuchs-Marx) reported that hers and Tony's health is pretty good; they both continue to play tennis and she does zumba and pilates. That said, Tony had had pain from shingles since April 2019 and Rosemary continues to live with Parkinson's, alleviated by medication. Their children and grandchildren have all acquired German citizenship to get European passports. Their granddaughter Molly, now 18, has started to study physics and philosophy at Bristol University. Their garden was productive in 2019 thanks to Tony's tender care, as well as the extra sunlight they were still getting from the absence of the Earl's Court building which used to shade it. To build the planned apartment blocks was still not financially viable. Their little nectarine tree produced about fifty delicious fruits. They have continued to travel for holidays and short breaks, by themselves or with friends or family, and have also been seeing friends and visitors. Sadly, three friends had died in the past year; they were getting to that age group. One was a former neighbour whom Rosemary first met when both of them were obviously pregnant in 1972. The year as a whole was overshadowed by the twists and turns of British politics. Rosemary was in contact with **Avril Goldstein (Le Tissier)**, whose husband of over fifty years, Eric, died in October just after his 90th birthday.

Bridget Towle had pencilled the reunion date of 16ᵗʰ May into her diary, commenting that sixty years was a frighteningly long time to retain such vivid memories of a school.

Barbara Workman (May)'s son had had three open heart operations to replace aortic and mitral valves, which was followed by a nasty infection and more hospital for nine weeks. It was all very touch and go and a nightmare of a time - very surreal - but thankfully he seemed to be good when she emailed.

Section 29 (1959)
Section Representative:
Myrth Russell (Hudson)

Joan Beckinsdale (Hills) Not too much to report really. Life pretty busy as usual. Still running church choir, local Mothers' Union branch and being PCC secretary. Since last summer our parish has been without a vicar (though hope for not much longer), so have also been drafted in to take the odd service. I do a good sung Matins.

Grandchildren all growing up fast. One has finished university, working for BBC, and three more started this year, plus one in sixth form doing A Levels, and the sixth one is busy training for the next Commonwealth Games.

Otherwise just feeling older and the joints creak a bit more, but still have time to enjoy a bit of serious gardening.

Sue Bowden (Humpidge) We continue in our tiny woodland cottage and still manage to enjoy our flocks of rare breed chickens and Shetland sheep. Our daughters together with eight grandchildren are both within an hour away. We regularly take the donkey to churches and schools and care homes, and he's still on the 'staff' of Gloucester Cathedral! (the donkey not Andrew!) Apart from being a bit creaky we're not bad for our age as they say, and very grateful for it.

Celebrated our golden wedding last year with a weekend thanksgiving party in the field to which three hundred friends came. An especial joy to see **Pricie** and **Libby Houston** - dear Westonbirt friends.

Living fairly close, we often go to watch grandchildren's sporting activities that take place in Westonbirt grounds which evoke many memories!

Helen Brown (Todd) We had a wonderful holiday to Australia last Autumn, exploring Western Australia and then city-hopping across the country visiting good friends. During the summer we had enjoyed visits from friends and family.

During the year two of our grandchildren became engaged, and we look forward to the first wedding in that generation in May. Our daughter Alison is now living a full and more active life thanks to the DBS surgery she underwent in 2018 for her Parkinson's disease. In October she held a party to celebrate her 55th birthday and the anniversary of her operation and almost the whole family were there plus friends from all periods of her life.

Another special occasion this year was when Philip and I met **Myrth** and Andy for lunch in Moffat, roughly halfway between our homes. We enjoyed exchanging reminiscences and photos. It was the first time we had met since leaving school in 1959!

Lin Coleman (Lavinia Hutton) I'm still working part-time as a psychotherapist, seeing individuals at home and couples at Tavistock Relationships in the centre of London. Difficult to retire completely but am slowly cutting down the work.

To relax, I enjoy doing patchwork, gardening, singing and have just begun to have Italian lessons in an attempt to improve my rusty conversational level. Trouble is, they all seem to speak English when we go for our annual 'Italy fix', so I doubt I'll get a chance to put anything into practice!

Angela Fenhalls (Allen) A busy year altering Victorian town house to cope with advancing age. A wonderful opportunity to clear junk and, although disruptive, better than moving. As a colleague said, one is lucky to be touched by the magic of Kew Gardens, and easy access is a must for me. Meandering through old photos has been fun too. Husband, Richard, continues to explore in old cars whilst I took the ageing body to Kazakhstan, near the Russian/Chinese border. To quote a botanical friend "if you go somewhere that is perfect, you are ten years too late." **Alex Pugh (Robertson)** was a welcome visitor.

Libby Houston This last year I've been ill, and my brother died - not sure if I can dig out anything jollier! But **Sue** and George - **Humpidge/Bowden** had a golden wedding weekend party - via a donkey cart! And yes, I am still working on ropes / cliffs, but nothing particularly exciting.

Linda Northcroft (Morley) A year of ups and downs, as for us all I expect. My two young dogs keep me exercising daily, which is good if sometimes exhausting. Daily life trundles on, but my health has not been so good this year, particularly breathing, as a cough has been disrupting, particularly to my choral society sessions and concerts, which has been disappointing. I still follow the political scene closely although I am no longer involved except as a Party member.

I've had three good escapes with my partner, to Madeira, Scotland and Israel. The visit to Israel was fascinating and most memorable as Granville and I became engaged to marry whilst there! I think this was a bit of a surprise to both of us at our great ages. Anyway, in for a penny, in for a pound, and we are getting married next month (March) in the village where I used to live.

As we both have a house, we shall probably continue commuting for the time being, but this will eventually have to be resolved. Meanwhile we enjoy our time together, both trying to comply with each other's wishes, as neither of us will obey the other, both being stubborn. Hopefully next year I will be around to give an update on this adventure! (My new name will be **Angell** and also Lady (of) Cannock - I am told not to forget that!)

Myrth Russell (Hudson) My news, annoyingly, is a slow cancer, an NET. Even though slow, I have to decide whether to go with starving the cells, juicing carrots, and drinking various teas, or the NHS medication. I hope your news is better.

The good news is that my children and three grandchildren are all OK. My grandson in the USA is doing theatre lighting design at UCLA; his younger sister is planning to come to University in GB, possibly Scotland, reading maths, (like my brother); and my local granddaughter is musical and making her way in the world by playing the clarsach (Gaelic harp) at events.

In September we took our American cousins on a week's tour round the Highlands. The trip was terrific, apart from the food, most of which was mediocre. Take warning, and plan around good food.

We are looking forward to a journey south based around the May 16th reunion. It is a good time to enjoy the beautiful western countryside, and to see old friends.

Section 28 (1958)
Section Representative:
Sue Hicks (Harker)

Thanks to all who replied this year. This is being compiled in extraordinary circumstances caused by COVID-19, which had hardly been mentioned a few weeks ago and is now a major concern worldwide. I wonder how Westonbirt is faring as schools shut down today.

Sheila Astbury (Stuart) Still playing tennis, but now in geriatric style, and it is much easier now I have had both eyes treated for cataracts. My son is now divorced, but the grandchildren split their time between the parents, so I am able to see them fairly often.

Last year I had a walking holiday in Austria near the Zugspitze and an interesting archaeological tour of Sicily in the autumn.

Jennie Bland (May) Like everyone else, I suppose, this is my 80th year but (other than more frequent visits to 'Delhi') I honestly don't feel any different.

I am very busy with a role in Canongate, my son's publishing house, and with my cookery school, Leiths, which has expanded and continues to lead the field. We pride ourselves on our professionalism – our graduates are in all the best restaurants in London as well as working as food journalists, designers, food photographers, book writers etc. We are also in 53 schools – Westonbirt was the first.

My eldest son is now 56; my newest, sixteenth, grandchild just two months old, so we are a wide-ranging family, with most of my grandchildren working through A Levels and universities or already involved in people-aware, valuable careers. A couple of times a year, we manage to get together for a few days, twenty-seven of us, and I am happy that this has meant that all the cousins know and love each other and meet up at other times. I fear that the world they all face is (thanks to the mess we've made of things) going to be pretty challenging and even threatening, so I am reassured to know that, when I snuff it, they will all support and care for each other, hopefully for generations. Isn't that what it's all about?

This will be a demanding year for me as after eighty years living almost exclusively in the country (in Ireland, at beautiful Westonbirt, in Hampshire), I am selling up and moving near to children in Notting Hill. I know it's the wise thing to do, but I really dread losing garden, rough walks, horses, friendly people, clean air - but it makes sense, and I certainly don't want my children to be landed with sorting out all the stuff I have gathered. It's the end of an era for sure, but I do love the theatre, galleries, lectures etc, so at least my mind will be active – I'll probably grow in spirit.

As I write, it is a heavenly spring day. From my window I can see mares and foals, two foxes about to climb to their lair in a lime tree (yes!), fighting pheasants, a muntjac, a forgotten football, and buds on the climbing roses. COVID-19 threat is approaching so I have (happily) put myself under house and garden arrest and plan to sort boxes, reread books which I won't be able to take to London, and paint.

Life has been good – those years at Westonbirt remain amongst my happiest. How lucky we were.

Sue Hicks (Harker) We celebrated our golden wedding and John's 80th birthday last Easter, with a party including my brother from New Zealand, a nephew from Canada, John's brother from France, our daughter and family from Ireland, and many others. Sadly, many relatives were too old or frail to travel. My own 80th party has been cancelled for now. I am so grateful for Skype and FaceTime so I can still see everybody even though we have scattered all over the world.

We did not go on holiday last year as I was suffering from a bad reaction to a medication which stole the summer, and now we are 'holidaying' at home. I am looking forward to having a perfect garden and spotless house and sorting out all the files and papers (I wish!) Until now I have been going to the usual round of concerts, drama productions, U3A groups, pilates, but life has suddenly changed totally as we await the onslaught of COVID-19. Sadly, my church of over thirty years has been disbanded, but a local Anglican church has been very welcoming, until it closed for the virus.

We have bought a small electric car (Renault Zoe), which is delightfully easy to drive and seems to be the way forward.

Anne Mercer (Seear) Has no spectacular news this year, just the normal round of events.

Lesley Scoular I have a chronic bronchial condition which sadly precludes me from climbing the hills any more, but am keeping as many other activities going as I can. I can't believe that I'll be 80 quite soon, but it must be true, as a number of my friends are there already! I'm still trying to learn to paint, but acknowledging I'll never be an artist.

Margaret Squires (Renshaw) Just the same old same old, as we continue to plod up hills. A friend booked a hunting lodge in May and husband and I climbed a Munro (A'Mhaighdean) for my 80th birthday. Apart from that, our attention turned to the Lake District where we had several separate weeks gradually (and very slowly) ticking off the Wainwrights. We went to Paris in 38°C to see grandson Joss graduate from Sciences Po (The Paris Institute of Political Studies), and he has a job at last. He lived with us for three or four years when he was a student at St Andrews, so we feel we know him best of the four grandchildren.

Catherine Whittingham (Norman Moses) This year has been busy: our granddaughter who has lived with us since she was a baby left home to go to university in Victoria, the other side of the country. She had a very unfortunate beginning: within the first two weeks she was involved in a bus crash while on a university trip. It was horrific, two students killed outright and many injured. It was a bad start. We flew to the west coast three times to see her. She is getting on, but it was very hard.

We have just sold our house and bought a condo. We are moving in May and because we will have about half the space, it means massive decluttering and getting rid of stuff. The rest of the family are all well, although my daughter-in-law Yuka broke her leg skiing in the back country and had to be helicoptered out. She runs a catering business which she has been running from her couch!

We didn't go anywhere very exciting last year after Portugal in March, although we had a few fun golfing holidays with friends. A lot of Canadians are refusing to go to the States while Trump is in office, and we feel the same. An American friend from medical school came to stay in October and she is heartbroken by the state of the country. I can still play golf although very badly.

I am still involved in the Grandmothers to Grandmothers group of the Steven Lewis Foundation, you may have heard of it because there is at least one group in the UK. Steven Lewis was the Canadian Ambassador to the UN in the seventies and became so appalled at the plight of orphans in sub-Saharan Africa he started this foundation. There are over a hundred groups of grandmothers across Canada and millions have been raised. It is amazing how much money can be generated in small ways. The money goes straight to the grandmothers caring for their children, without government intervention, and has allowed them to become politically active and make changes. I am the treasurer, not that I have any accounting experience, but I can still add up and keep the books in an amateur fashion.

Sections 25, 26 & 27 (1955, 1956 and 1957)
Section Representative:
Angela Potter (Tracy)

It is Easter Monday today and I simply cannot imagine what the world will be like when you read this. Will it be looking forward to normality, or spiralling down to a doomsday scenario? In the few weeks since sending out the request for news, our lives have changed dramatically, and even the most interesting news dulls in comparison. Most of my correspondents answered promptly, so I'm afraid there are a great many lovely plans of weddings, anniversary celebrations and holidays that will have had to have been cancelled or deferred. I hope, like me, that everyone is finding the enforced leisure a useful opportunity to catch up with all those abandoned New Year resolutions.

Like many of us, I too am now 80, so I have a lifetime of unfinished chores, but I did have a special surprise birthday weekend in April 2019 with nine members of our immediate family - in Prague! Last autumn we went on safari in Zambia, with our eldest son and daughter-in-law – what a fantastic experience! We would gladly go back if it wasn't for the tedious journey to get there. This summer there was going to be a family party here to jointly celebrate two 18th , three 21st, one 50th and two 80th birthdays, plus one 25th wedding anniversary! Ah well, less work for me!

The news from Westonbirt (which my Sections already know) is that the Holford Trust have been awarded a modest grant from the Heritage Lottery Fund, which will mainly be used for the partial restoration of some of the Westonbirt garden features – the Italian Garden gazebos, fountains and the stone seats. The lake too is likely to be restored soon thanks to a very generous donation from an Old Girl.

I've recently heard that **Ann Williamson** is suffering from dementia and is now in a care home near Warwick. I understand she has settled in well. If anyone wants her address, please contact me via the school. I know of two deaths that have occurred this last year – **Pauline Hathorn (Horrocks)**, and **Angela Knapp (Boswell)** both of whom left in 1957.

Section 27 (1957)

Joan Allan (Blakeborough) This last year has been one of big birthdays. Our eldest grandson, Nick's son, Cameron, was 18 in March. He has now left school and is at Manchester University. I reached 80 last April and Hugo and Katie celebrated turning 50 in September, Douglas was 80 on 1st November and had said he wanted no party or celebration. However, I think he felt a bit sad as the day approached. Unknown to him, Colin and family had secretly arranged to come from Trinidad. When the doorbell rang and they walked in, Douglas's face was a picture. The surprise was total and the very best present he could have had.

In June we spent a few days in Shetland with friends. We were surprised at the prosperity of the Islands compared to other parts of Scotland, all due to the Sullom Voe oil and gas refinery, of course. Then in late July we had a week in Sutherland at Clashnessie, near Lochinver, Finally, in December, we flew to Port of Spain, Trinidad, to spend Christmas and New Year with Colin and family. They have a lovely house with lots of space and a large pool in the garden. A very different posting from Baku, although they much enjoyed their five years in Azerbaijan and, due to social media, they still keep up with all their friends there.

I continue to play bad golf occasionally, but much prefer the good bridge we have here. We also continue to be active in the local Anglican/Methodist church, but no longer have a house group as the members all either returned to the UK, died, or were unable to stay awake for more than five minutes to watch a forty-minute DVD. We now attend an evening group where the DVD is much shorter!

I spent a weekend with my sister, **Helen Lilley (Blakeborough)**, in August, while her family were away. Despite being diagnosed with Alzheimer's, she still manages to remain in her own home. She was upset to have her driving licence removed, but it was not before time. With some outside help, her daughter, Cathryn, is amazing. She has her mother organised so that she can cope safely at home. Her two sons put Granny's pills ready for the morning while she is surreptitiously cooking the evening meal at the same time. Helen blew up the kitchen, hence why meals are now ready made.

Barbara Anderson (Tucker) Like many of our year, I have now become an octogenarian! My 80th birthday was three weeks ago, and I celebrated it with a lunch party. On the actual day I was invited as a guest to a day of 'Expedition Medicine' for retired members of the Royal College of Physicians. Lectures ranged from crossing the Antarctic to climbing in the Andes and Himalayas 'researching the cause of altitude sickness'. Expedition medicine had been one of my special interests when I was working in a university health service. It was a fascinating day – and, at my age, all the better for enjoying it from a comfortable chair!

I still work two half days a week for the charity Hope and Homes for Children, doing filing, archiving and writing thank-you letters for donations. I belong to our local U3A and host a creative writing group (some time ago I wrote an essay on Westonbirt for the group*). (Editor's note: This essay will form part of the Association's 90th celebrations, to be re-scheduled for 2021.)* I am half-heartedly looking for a retirement flat, as the day will come when I can no longer manage a three-floor house with a sloping garden, but I'm in no hurry to move.

Priscilla Boddington (Pentreath) I don't really have much news. Last year I had a wonderful week's cruise on a clipper ship in the Mediterranean with my brother, whose wife had just died. A month later he also died, and just before his memorial service in the chapel at Greenwich (where he had once been captain of the naval college), my other brother died, too. So quite a year. This year has got off to a better start with the wedding of my oldest granddaughter, and later this month I shall go to Dartmoor for the christening of my step-great-grandson. I'm so lucky to have a very supportive family.

Judith Briggs (Walker) My news is somewhat sparse this year. We are thankful to be able to get about and travel around and plan to visit the family in America at the end of May for our eldest grandchild's high school graduation - a big event there - so we are looking forward to that; and then getting both families together for a week in Dorset at the end of June for an advance celebration of my 80th birthday. Like everyone else I can hardly believe it!

Here we continue to visit the Game Reserve area in South Africa, which we much enjoy, as well as the Cape where Guy and Kate live with their two children, Anna (14) and Oliver (11). At home I continue to assist with various local activities and try to keep as active as possible, with pilates etc, and a walking group. We enjoy the Symphony Orchestra concerts. We are fortunate to have quite a bit going on, and are able to attend various talks and concerts and enjoy our house and garden. Politics still absorbs me though I am not as involved as I was, but I keep in touch through the committee of the local branch of the Democratic Alliance. The country lurches from crisis to crisis, and our electricity is far from reliable, so a good stock of lamps and candles is always to hand! Much corruption is exposed but the culprits not brought to book. When something becomes endemic it is difficult to get rid of it.

Christabel Cumberlege (Jacques) I blame it on the weather and our planned house move next July, but I have been completely deprived of inspiration. I will of course let you know our new address. Luckily, we will still be in our lovely village. The thought of walking to the post office and not seeing any familiar faces or being able to pop round to our fantastic village stores without being deprived of lovely country walks was too strong, so we are staying put. I am glad to have had so many lovely memories of Westonbirt, mainly the trees and gardens, and of course, friends.

Gillie Drake (Strain) I don't have much news other than seeing our family (four married grown-up children) and our eight grandchildren ranging from 9 up to uni. Jonathan, our eldest, lives in Sydney and has had months of smoky air. They went to their beach house in NSW over Christmas and New Year and spent most of their time sweeping hot burning ash off their property. They were lucky as the wind changed direction when they were just getting really worried.

So glad to hear about the lottery grant. It is really good to think of the Italian Gardens being restored. I don't think we ever did anything to help towards their beauty by playing tag over the stonework! We had such fun too, turning the fountains on to unsuspecting people! Also, I was very sad the last time I was there to see the lake empty and forlorn and remember skating on it in my mother's brown skating boots in the days when we had cold winters. Our garden here in Guernsey could do with some real cold weather to kill the bugs, not this endless rain and wind. Even our Silver Sebrights hate it and stay in their hutch.

Vanessa Evans (Llewelyn) My 80th birthday is this March. I live in San Diego, California USA - have done since 1965. I am still working three half days a week as an orthoptist, giving eye exercises to children and adults, and I love it. I live with my husband. My son lives in Berlin Germany, my daughter lives in New Orleans, USA. I have five recorder music students that I teach music to in my house and belong to two recorder social quartets. I go to yoga classes twice week, swim once a week, and belong to two knitting groups. I nearly forgot the singing group I sing in one evening a week. All this as a result of my wonderful education at Westonbirt. I have three photos of Westonbirt up in my living room.

Rowena Ginns (Cullin) Sorry for such a late response caused by a health scare which fortunately had a positive outcome. Just before the coronavirus hit, we had a weekend in London with eight of our American Coaching friends, dinner at the Churchill War Rooms, lunches, exhibitions, very full on as ever but very enjoyable. All returned safe and sound before the lock down. We feel fortunate to be in the country with a large garden and helpful people to shop for us. We should have been on a Mediterranean cruise which would have been lovely, cancelled of course as no doubt will be Ascot and all the ongoing horse activities even into September. A family gathering for Bill's 80th birthday is now a non-event, various members being locked down in Hong Kong, London and the New Forest. We hope we shall all come through this before too long.

Jennifer Grant Rennick (Lang) Everything has drastically changed since your plea for news! Now I have more than enough time to supply you with something thanks to coronavirus! Now that the great 90th birthday party has been put off for a year I might be able to rouse some of us old girls who are still left to make a stab at it then!

Otherwise my news is much the same. Living in Tetbury suits me well, even in this extraordinary time. Each week our parameters get narrower. Food is a constant challenge. I am lucky enough to have willing friends offering to help, and my Russian tenant in my house next door is willing to do anything. But it is hard to leave the shopping to others.

Bridge has been my social saviour up to now, and I have many different fours which kept me busy and stimulated. Now that has had to be put on hold, and I am too much of a Luddite to want to learn how to play it online! So, I am concentrating on a story about my life which is keeping me entertained and hopefully will eventually be able to be read by my friends and family.

Jane McCarthy (Hellyer) My main news is that my best friend from Westonbirt, **Angela Knapp (Boswell)**, died of cancer in October, having had a hard time - but after an exciting life. I knew she was very ill the previous Christmas and didn't send a Christmas card. Suddenly the telephone rang mid- afternoon, and a giggling voice said, "you thought I was dead and buried". It was Angela and we had a long conversation. She was never one to join the 'Westonbirt' anything!

But she and Michael were kind enough to invite me, on several occasions, to Highclere to watch the yearlings paraded (which they have been involved with for eons), then it all stopped when *Downton Abbey* started filming, and they were not allowed to bring guests. Having been involved with racing for most of my life (not to their standard!), I now have reached the depths and belong to a thing called ELITE (with thousands of members!) I am mainly interested in their breeding – seven brood mares, but a lot of flat horses. I am really interested in 'jumpers', but it makes a nice relaxing afternoon watching them race – on the TV! What an exciting life! Given up travelling, though I keep promising myself that I will go back to Zimbabwe – one more time!

Alison Reed (Hill) As Anthony died just before Christmas, the last couple of months have been a time of readjustment. Sad as it was, I could not have wished for him to struggle on any longer. And I was glad that he was able to be at home. I am being kept busy with wonderful support from friends, Westonbirt friends very much included. In early May I am going on a bird-watching cruise from Plymouth to Oban, calling in at different places every day, including the Scilly Isles and various ports of call off the west coast of Ireland as well as St Kilda – all weather permitting and hoping for no more devastating storms.

Madeline Williamson (Langford) John has difficulty walking *(he has Parkinson's AP)* and I can't leave him on his own overnight, which slows our life down somewhat; however, I am well, which is a good thing in the circumstances! I meet up in London with **Alison Reed (Hill)** and **Charlotte Graves-Taylor** from time to time and also went to Anthony's funeral. **Rachel Palmer (Phillips), Di Ashby (Carolin)** and **Fiona Holland (Love)** were there too.

Section 26 (1956)

Felicity Coulthard (Scott) Most recent excitements have been the storms, our river reached the front door but didn't enter. What a terrible time others have endured. Our practice nurse told me the human body is not designed to live into its eighties. Mine now has arthritis everywhere, and I am one of the lucky ones. I can still drive and give lifts to the less fortunate. I still live in my home of 64 years and my son and his family live next door. I belong to all sorts of classes and groups. I am not a Merry Widow, but I am a very happy one. Last July I visited Westonbirt and strolled round the garden. It all looked much as I remember it! I also went to the arboretum, which is much more commercialised these days. The trees are still beautiful.

Jane Hancock (Quale) We have just returned from three weeks cruising in the Caribbean: hot and mostly sunny all the time, while the UK was having rain, gales and more rain, so we were very fortunate. We are very lucky as we are comparatively fit and mobile compared to many of our friends and relations, consequently our children are encouraging us to travel as much as possible while we still can. So, we are off back to the Caribbean mid-March. This time we shall be coming back by ship trans-Atlantic, as we are not good at jet lag. We have another two cruises booked for later in the year.

It is now five years since our granddaughter, Chloe, had her malignant brain tumour removed, and she is doing remarkably well. We cannot thank GOSH (Great Ormond Street Hospital) enough for all the marvellous care and attention she has been given. It will be her sixth birthday in a week's time - a milestone we thought she might never reach. The rest of our family are fit and flourishing.

Margaret Jackson (Grubb) I don't really keep in touch with Westonbirt people/happenings. I live in the wrong place and move in a totally different world! I do keep up (just!) with **Rachel Palmer (Phillips),** usually visiting her in London between visiting elder daughter in Berkhamsted and younger daughter in Sevenoaks. I have recently reconnected with **Cyrilla Potter (Monk).** She lives in Salisbury and we go there once a year. Over the years I have seen **Patsy (Toh)** occasionally – I look her up on the internet from time to time – only a few years ago she was still professor of piano at the Royal Academy. *(She is still on the staff list of the Purcell School AP).*

Cyrilla Potter (Monk) For me being eighty is the new sixty. I am having fun. In the last twelve months I have been to Long Island, New York, five times! My book of poems is to be published at some point. I'm still writing *My Life* but it takes so long, the research for it is fascinating but time-consuming! **Veronica Graham Brown (Howarth)** and I keep in touch. I am hoping **Margaret Jackson (Grubb)** will be able to visit me again this summer.

Anne Renard (Matthews) Parkinson's and bad eyesight are making using a computer difficult. I have had a very frustrating year, waiting for a broken leg to heal, including three months in a care home. I'm still unable to walk properly again, so no trips and holidays, or news to pass on. Hope 2020 will be kind to us all.

A late extra! We had a visit from **Flicka Coulthard** yesterday. Several years since we have seen her, and we had a good catch-up. She was the person through whom Chris and I met, many years ago.

Oriel Rogers-Coltman (Corbett) Life in Shropshire has been changed somewhat by the acquisition of a Border Terrier puppy last July. She joins our elderly friend who will be 14 in April and who is starting to show her age. Another landmark in April will be our diamond wedding anniversary. We are having a celebration at the end of May when hopefully summer will have arrived. Our kind daughter and son-in-law are hosting it. Apart from that our grandchildren have almost all finished school - only one left there after the summer term - one gainfully employed, five at university, one on a gap year.

Section 25 (1955)

Beth Barrington-Haynes (Elizabeth) Looking back to highlights (and a low one), I recall another superb service in St George's Chapel (two choirs!) and champagne reception in Windsor Castle, hosted every four years by the Queen for members of the Royal Victorian Order. Splendid procession of royals and a few dignitaries, in colourful robes. Robust singing until second verse of the National Anthem when significantly less - congregation short on the words and embarrassed to read them.

Soon I was off to Lakes Maggiore and Como for a memorably enchanting holiday visiting, with expert guides, Renaissance villas and vast acres of gardens, which are many and wondrous, as are the lakes too. Our second hotel was an historic villa with its equally famous, steep, formal gardens. Living in London next to the Hurlingham Club means enjoying its beautifully kept gardens plus the chance to entertain friends without washing up! It's good to have re-connected to **Alyn Denholm (Paisley)**. **Bridget Frost (Kell)** has moved here and refurbished her flat most appealingly.

Christmas with brother and most of his family, though Nicholas went to Garda with his fiancée whose parents live there. We went to the long, spectacular music and light show early one dark evening at Stourhead.

Back in October I was diagnosed with incurable lung cancer so am now 'on' immunotherapy, which is OK, although side effects are many and varied. Friends are remarkably supportive, offering shopping etc. but I am 100% mobile so not required... yet.

Patricia (Puff) Drew Yes, I'm still alive!! And still making art.

Bridget Frost (Kell) This news has a sadness to it, as my sister, Virginia, died last September. Her cancer had returned and although she had managed to hold it back for three years and lead a full life, it just wasn't to be. Out of the four girls, **Caroline Fuchs (Kell)** and I remain. On a lighter note, as we have so far died from the bottom up, I am the next!

I travelled a lot last year - too much in fact - but all most enjoyable. Perhaps I mentioned Caroline and I visiting our cousin in Thailand last February? A highlight was a week's cruise through the Norwegian fjords with my daughter, Laura and her two children: very beautiful. Also, a visit to my army son in Canada as well as an annual stay in our family house in France.

Heather Owen very kindly asked me to join her and friends in her stepdaughter's beautiful chateau in the south of France. So, you see I have been rather spoiled. And finally, a wonderful week with my sister Caroline and friends at Bagno Vignoni - a spa up in the Tuscan hills. Good news: Caroline is coming to live in Rivermead Court, just across the car park from me. She will have said more in her own news. It is also a bonus to have **Beth Barrington-Haynes** across the way from me. Westonbirt is still flying the flag. I have also been in touch with **Jennie Bland (May).** So, all good.

Jill Gibson (Connor) I have no special news - life continues much as usual with home and family, Church and village occupying much time. We continue holidaying in Arran but now going at different times of the year and it is interesting to see the island at different seasons; yellow flag iris all along one part of the coastal road in spring (we had only seen the dead stems in summer) and the many seals that haunt the south coast providing entertaining viewing. We plan on revisiting Croatia for a bit of sunshine in the autumn and are starting to plan a trip to visit Canada next year when our eldest son Douglas will be taking up a post in Ottawa for three years.

Veronica Graham Brown (Howarth) I had a full knee replacement last July, which took a while to get over... very painful but necessary exercises afterwards. I had two hip replacements about fourteen years ago, but the knee surgery is something I would not like to repeat. However, it was successful, and I can enjoy walking once again. I now have ten grandchildren. One of my granddaughters is getting married at the end of June, and I am very much looking forward to the occasion.

Patricia Hedges (Crowe) My book *The Raj, the Rolls and the Remorse* is doing well, and I have had lots of people getting in touch with me - Indians, Anglo-Indians, and many others, it has been very rewarding. I have been to Italy a lot this year, to Florence and Lake Iseo. I have a friend there with a Newfoundland dog, and of course a car which means he can drive me around, and we have also visited Pisa, Lucca and Lake Garda. At home I am involved with four French-speaking groups (I was amazed to find these in Torquay). I also go to Mensa meetings. About twenty-five years ago I did a big research project involving nearly three thousand members. I hope to read news from my contemporaries at school - this is a distant memory now, although I went back about fifteen years ago to talk to the girls doing psychology.

Alison Maguire (Mason) I have travelled a lot in the last year, ending up with a trip to Hawaii with the International Dendrologist Society. I have just returned after fourteen days walking volcanoes and craters, following trails up to waterfalls, swimming on the edge of the massive surf and seeing extraordinary trees not seen at Westonbirt yet. Otherwise, life goes on mostly in Scotland, but every month a few days in London; in this way I do manage to see both sons and their wives and children. Mat is still working to save the planet and we have installed a ground-sourced heat pump in Scotland. Edward has his architectural practice in London and is involved with building hospitals.

Section 24 (1954)
Section Representative:
Alison Robinson (De Courcy-Ireland)

I continue to be grateful to all of those who respond to my pleas for news. As always I am impressed by the amount of your activity - learning new languages and travelling the world, as well as helping with grandchildren (and even great-grandchildren) and being stoical about the aches and pains that increasingly plague us and will sadly prevent many of us attending the 90th birthday celebrations.

Elizabeth Bennett (Anning) says she is still around and enjoying what she can still do. She reads avidly, especially enjoying a good thriller! She says she becomes positively obsessive about thousand-piece jigsaws. 'I am on my way to bed, trying to see if one piece might just fit ... and before I know it, two hours have passed...' Elizabeth also does needlepoint, visits her son and his wife in the Perigourd Vert and feels she can cope with most of what old age throws at her, but finds the hardest part is the loss of old friends, leaving huge gaps in one's life.

Elizabeth Ells (Rawlence) sent a message via her sister **Mary Cave** to say she is still living in Canada north of Ottawa and it was extremely cold.

Amelia Gardener (Langford) feels she is getting rather doddery but is still alive and reasonably active with the help of her carer husband Ian who does all the shopping and many other things. The undoubted highlight of their past year was the arrival of a parcel from South Korea on Ian's 85th birthday in April. It contained a printed copy of the Abuan Bible (on which Ian worked for many years) with a fine oxblood red cover. Five thousand copies were sent directly to Abua in the Niger Delta near Port Harcourt, where a ceremony of dedication was held on December 28th on the local football ground. They have been emailed videos of this colourful occasion and were particularly excited to see the massed choirs of many denominations from all over the area. Recently Amelia was alarmed when **Margot Gill (Wilcox)** phoned to say she had been unable to contact **Jane Sutton**. Fortunately, when Amelia phoned Jane, she found her not only very much alive, but recently returned from a trip to the Canadian Arctic and still taking church services!

Anna Grange (Hetherington) writes that 'Age is creeping up, but apart from a spell of polymyalgia all is good. After twenty-five years she has given up doing the flowers in Malmesbury Abbey, which was sad, but such a relief not to carry bowls of soggy oasis up and down the aisle. Anna is still involved with her daughters in conservation, planting more trees and they have got three belted Galloways to replace sheep on the fell. The boggy flowers and sedges are returning in greater numbers. Anna enjoys Malmesbury's wonderful theatre group, with monthly visits to places such as Stratford, and particularly appreciates the joy of a coach waiting at the end of the performance. Her eldest granddaughter got married in June, and they had a lovely international gathering on the banks of the Dordogne, but Anna found it rather a shock to be the oldest person there!

Janet Knight (Sykes) says she is slowing down these days and the weather does not help. Fortunately, her house is not near the River Severn but nevertheless she has had her garden and cellar flooded, and even had small frogs swimming in the latter! Janet regretted that she would not be able to come to the 90th anniversary but sends her best wishes to everyone and says she 'would love to hear from anyone who remembers Sedgwick in 1947 and Gloucester thereafter'.

Sheena Mackenzie replied to the request for news within minutes of receiving it which earned her maximum brownie points from her Section Rep! She too says she is still alive but no longer wishes to do any travelling! Sadly, she had heard **Fiona Gray (Inskip)** is now in a nursing home, still healthy other than suffering from the dreaded Alzheimer's. Sheena herself was hospitalized over Christmas and New Year with diverticulitis, which scared her children since she had never really been ill before, but it had a wonderful effect on her aloof cat! 'When I came home she meowed at me for nearly half an hour, and since then has morphed into an affectionate cat, following me from room to room!'

Valerie Moorby (Holmes-Johnson) was looking forward to the imminent arrival of a new great-grand-child when she wrote. She comments that she keeps pretty well and certainly busy. She has started a new French conversation class with a view to brushing up her very rusty French before the end of May, when her youngest and his fiancée are getting married in France. They actually live in San Francisco, so, with many family members and a lot of American friends expected, they have taken a chateau in the Loire valley and are looking forward to a great time. (Valerie's only trip abroad last year was to go with them to see the venue, hence the discovery of the rustiness of her French!) Her other family excitement last year was her younger granddaughter's wedding in September, which was lovely, the occasion completely stolen by their baby! Valerie comments, 'How times change!' She adds that she is hoping to see **Mary Rusinow** in September, but otherwise life is all very domestic and by no means earth shattering. Helmsley continues to be a good place to live with lots going on: Arts Centre , Musical Festivals etc, so with all that and the fact that she has so far managed to stay in her home, albeit with help in the garden, she feels she is very lucky.

Heather Owen (Grange) is looking forward to the 90th anniversary celebrations. She comments that, for all the present concern about climate change, Cornwall has always had rainy winters. Among the highlights of Heather's year were the village commemorations of the 75th anniversary of the D-Day landings, with displays of photographs, uniforms, kitbags, medals, maps, recipes and much memorabilia as well as military vehicles, including a jeep. A local resident, now aged 97 and still fit and spruce, had taken part, and many military personnel, including American forces, had embarked from Falmouth, which made remembering especially meaningful.

Heather comments if any of us (octogenarians or younger) think of writing our memoirs, she can thoroughly recommend a memoir writing course she recently attended at the East India Club, organised by *The Oldie* magazine, with erudite and distinguished speakers. Now it is down to the hard work of getting it on to paper!

Alison Robinson (de Courcy-Ireland) has had a year somewhat dominated by family dramas and writes 'With a family as large as ours, someone is always having (or think they are having) a crisis of one sort or another! And, while we cannot pretend to be as intrepid travellers as some of our section, we have managed trips to Antwerp (for a granddaughter's graduation), to Dubai (to visit my son who is working there), and a fascinating cruise up the Dalmation Coast in a boat small enough to get into the less touristy harbours. Douglas has been diagnosed with a form of Parkinson's, but it is in the very early stages, and the medication is proving effective, so it doesn't pose too much of a problem so far. Meanwhile we both keep busy with village affairs and other interests, while being acutely aware that we are attending an increasing number of funerals and/or visiting old friends in their care homes. Like Elizabeth Bennett said above, that is the hardest part of getting older.'

Mary Rusinow (Worthington) commented that 2019 was fairly busy. This seemed an understatement in view of what followed. She writes: 'Christmas 2018 was in Pretoria as my son-in-law was appointed UNICEF representative for South Africa. On my return to Florida I saw an ad for cruises to Cuba, so I went. We only had one day there, but my friends had reserved a 1956 Cadillac, so we travelled around, for far too brief a time, in style! The next trip was to the Galapagos as I had promised such a trip to my granddaughter if she got into Oxford. She did and is now at Balliol. I went then to Italy but headed back to New York to hear grandson Kiran speak in the General Assembly at his graduation. He has gone to Duke. Back to Italy for the usual summer activities, broken by a party on Exmoor for elder daughter's 50th. September brought a trip down the Danube to places that I had seen in 1989; they have changed a bit. Christmas 2019 was in Johannesburg, but sadly son- in-law has been promoted by UNICEF and has had to go back to New York. Tamara will follow when Kofi finishes the school year. Alison is also moving, to the Hague. She is staying with the Dutch NGO that she has been with in Hanoi but will be a little closer to home. Probably 2020 will be calmer but I am off to South Africa for a family wedding at Easter.' *(Phew!!)*

Gillian Sandeman (Wright) is another inveterate globetrotter. Last July she and Sandy made a trip to the Pantanal region of Brazil. They travelled with a group of English friends with whom they had been on previous wildlife viewing trips. The Pantanal is the world's largest wetland, about 200,000 sq km. 'We went in the dry season when the floods have receded, and the wildlife is concentrated. That part of Brazil is cattle-ranching country, and we stayed on ranches that have recognized the value of eco-tourism and opened lodges on their properties. We walked, rode high viewing vehicles and went on boats in search of the abundant birds and mammals. Our little group of eight saw 209 bird species in twelve days – everything from tiny brown things on distant branches to flamboyant parakeets, toucans and macaws. Masses of mammals too: many jaguars (best seen from the water), ocelots, the ridiculous giant ant-eaters, capybaras, coati-mundi, deer, monkeys and more.'

She continues: 'We were in England and Scotland in October visiting family, including two great-granddaughters, and friends; then, in November, we had a nostalgic trip back to Neuchatel, where we spent the first penniless months of our marriage. So penniless that we rented the bedroom of our one-bedroom flat to a student. This time we stayed in a lakefront hotel. Then on to Zurich and Lucerne and a cruise down the Rhine. The cruise-boat captain was younger than some of our grandchildren.

'Since then we've been enjoying a relatively mild and snow-free winter, but I still miss snowdrops which won't appear here until April. We're going to Cyprus for more birds, flowers and butterflies with the same group in early April. We keep thinking we're too old to travel but keep doing it anyway – hoping for Indian wildlife next February! We also keep busy at home. My 87-year-old husband is still doing research and will be giving a paper at a big Coral Reef Symposium in Bremen in June. I enjoy serving on a couple of boards, including our local library board. Libraries are increasingly becoming free community resources where everyone is welcome. We even had homeless people sleeping in a big meeting room while the regular drop-in overnight shelter was being refurbished.'

Section 23 (1953)
Section Representative:
Jean Stone (Borritt)

Unfortunately, I have lost touch with some members of this section as e-mail addresses provided are no longer current.

Moira Gilbert (Melvin) kindly replied and apologised that she did not feel able to face the travel to the 90th birthday celebrations for the Association. Happily, she had managed a short spring break to a delightful family hotel in North Yorkshire, where the weather was unseasonably warm. The family keeps Moira occupied with their interests. She writes 'The eldest grand-daughter goes to kick boxing, which is a good hobby in this day and age. Hopefully it will not be needed. Her sister is keen on tennis, as I was at Westonbirt, and afterwards, until golf took over. My husband Peter still plays golf but now has to use a buggy to get around the course.'

Ann Greenstreet (Selby) Sorry not to have sent news for a while. We live very quietly as Anthony is 91 and rather lame. I still drive, but only locally – my eyes have been a problem, but I am now seeing better after two cataract operations. I also have to have injections most months to treat macular degeneration – the miracles of modern science. I enjoy U3A and the Arts Society (formerly NADFAS) and we are lucky in having good neighbours and living conveniently close to shops etc. The family live in the Twickenham area, and we see them all often. Rosanna writes for the *Guardian* and *Mail*, as well as editing the local Elmbridge magazine, which Miranda also writes for. Jane's family are all very sporty, including Lizzie, who has cystic fibrosis. She has just been put on a new 'wonder drug' and hopes to do sport sciences at university. Nine grandchildren, age range ten to twenty-two, keep us interested. Georgina got a first at Manchester and seems very highly paid in IT, Charlotte (21) lives in France, and all the others are still at school.

Section 21 & 22 (1951 & 1952)

Section Representative:
Margot Gill (Wilcox)

Margot Gill (Wilcox) Firstly, many thanks to those of you who replied, much appreciated. My year has disappeared in a flash. Not much travelling – Scotland for Stepma's funeral, Tetbury of course, for the Association day (not many of our year there!), Shell Pensioners Chairman's conference, cruise to the Canaries and a final one this year to France for a knee replacement. Knee doing very well, and I do not need a stick, hooray!

Obviously the present situation has curtailed many of our activities and travel plans. I am lucky not to be bored. There is so much to do that I do not miss company, but then I do have my dog, who answers back, it seems. May you all stay safe.

Lady Henniker (Julia Masson) I had a stroke in September 2016, and it has left me unable to walk and no movement down my left side. It is difficult to write or send emails these days because of my impaired vision. I no longer live in the Red House but in a residential care home. The carers are all very lovely, but it is not the same as being in my own home. I am also very lucky to have a personal assistant, Tracey; she is with me in the home five days a week. She is also my chauffeur, and we are out often even if it is just for a leisurely drive in the countryside.

My three daughters are all fine. Caroline, my eldest, lives in Portugal with her youngest daughter, Lucy, and they run an Airbnb, which attracts a lot of walkers who enjoy visiting for the birds and wildlife.

Caroline's eldest daughter, Amy, lives in Manchester with husband Ricardo and my two great grandchildren, Xavier (5) and Magda (2). My other granddaughter, Lottie May, lives in Portugal and runs her own language teaching school.

Victoria, my middle daughter, lives in Northumberland with her cat Bellamy, two rabbits and her three rescue hens! Ate, my youngest, lives and works in London. She works a lot with the council to make communal gardens in parks and empty spaces in London's Hackney area. She also teaches refugees.

I am lucky to have ten great-grandchildren through my two marriages. I hope that all is well with everyone.

Susan Kavanagh (Harris) For the most part I continue to live in the UK with my youngest daughter, Celia, and her family – never a dull moment with the comings and goings of the two girls. Aby (20) is now in her third year at university, studying Italian in Italy this year, while Audra (18) starts at Bath University in the fall. These two will be linking up with Victoria (22) who will be in Europe in early April for a three-month visit. Nathan (26) is serving with the US army in the Middle East, while Anthony (24) is now in the Philippines on an extended visit where he hopes to put his nursing skills to good practice.

I return to California mid-March for a couple of months, where business (tax season, etc) combines with pleasure. Linking up with family and friends there is always a joy, while being back with the Hispanic ministry that has been an important part of my life for some forty years is most special. During this visit I may be back in Mexico for few days. Life continues to be full of adventures.

Then I'd like to add that I continue to see **Mary Hall (Sercombe)** each visit. She and husband Bill celebrated their 60th wedding anniversary on January 2[nd.] Theirs is a very happy marriage. Daughter, Wendy, lives close by; she has two grand-daughters and teaches harp, plus keeping an eye on her parents.

Ann Parsons (Leighton) Haven't done much this year as I had a nasty fall in 2018 when I broke my femur. It has taken a long time to be able to walk again, but things are improving, although I'm still rather disabled. I am able to drive, and get about using two sticks. Have lots of lovely visitors, but most friends are of a similar age and we all have our aches and pains.

Ann Sadler (Millard) I can't think of anything to say, my days seem to follow a set pattern of table tennis, visiting the 'elderly' (those who are even older than me but possibly less agile!), running a village coffee morning, doing various odd jobs for the village church and singing in a choir – to name most of what I do. I am lucky to be reasonably fit, a bit arthritic and in need of hearing aids, but on the whole I don't have much to complain about.

Jane Sutton is still very much with us, travelling a great deal and as a licensed lay minister is kept busy, not only within the Anglican diocese but also helping with the local Methodists.

Section 19 & 20 (1949-50)
Section Representative:
Serena Jones

Sarah Abel (Poynor) I try and keep as active as I can, going for a walk each day and joining in with keep fit and art for memory classes. My family are very good to me and I have visited Maastricht, Luxembourg, and Nottingham, and went on a wonderful Mediterranean cruise. I am lucky to be able to look after myself and my house unaided.

Sue Gardiner-Hill (Strachan) Sue sent me a note last November thanking me for keeping in touch and saying that she was very happy at Westonbirt and grateful for the excellent education she had. Her writing was very legible, but she did explain that she is too old and lives too far away to come to events at the school.

Meriel Pickett (Sharpe) Such news as I have has been overtaken by the sudden and unexpected death of the eldest of our four sons on 1st February. He died of a massive heart attack, with no previous signs or symptoms, aged 59, leaving two much loved children from Amelia's first marriage and two boys barely in their teens. I was in Hungary with Ben's widow *(Ben was Meriel's third son, who died two years ago - SJ)* and her three children when this happened. Archie and Alex were the same age that Nylle and Leon are now, when Ben died.

Elizabeth Wells (Burt) Another year with grandchildren and great-grandchildren from overseas coming to stay, which is lovely for me. Irish granddaughter is now in London and was here whilst organising a flat. Otherwise a rather dull year in which I have slowed down and far too often leave it until tomorrow.

Elizabeth Wicks (Butcher) I feel very lucky that I am still able to drive, although smart motorways have put me off driving on those roads.

Frequent visits to the opera and ballet shown on the big screen are a joy, and I am still able to enjoy walks in the countryside and go to pilates classes. Lalu and Jo, my daughters, are wonderful – one is in London and the other in Taunton, and we are able to exchange visits. My grandson had a glorious wedding last August.

I realise I am lucky that life has been kind to me. I am in touch with **Anne Renard**, who has a tough time with Parkinson's Disease.

Joy Willey (Crowe) It's sometime since I sent in any News, and nothing really has changed. I find I spend more and more time with my family. So fortunate to have them all in the UK (except for granddaughter at Leiden University). Living near central London is an attraction for teenage granddaughters!

I continue to have close contact with Westonbirt as I still have one granddaughter at the school in Year 12 (lower sixth). They work so hard now. She is a keen lacrosse player, also playing for Scotland, and I am hoping to cheer them on at the National Schools Tournament at the end of February. She is full of hope they may do even better than last year. I certainly can't remember early morning practices in my day!

Sadly, many of my contemporaries are no longer around, but I spent the day with **Sylvia McDougall (Field)** at her house in Majorca last year. Since her husband died, she no longer comes to England as she has very little mobility. I had a phone conversation with **Elisabeth Wells (Burt)** at Christmas, and we intend to meet one day. I miss **June Jacobs (Caller)** since she died, as we met and talked regularly. An amazing person who achieved more internationally than I think any other of our generation. A June Jacobs Memorial lecture is being held in March at which a leading human rights activist will be the speaker. (*Editor's note: I was prompted by this to find out more about June Jacobs and her remarkable achievements.*)

Fortunately, I am still able to travel abroad - sadly no longer independent wanderings, but river cruises are better than nothing.

I continue to lobby without success to have an Old Girls meeting in London as I am sure others like me find the drive down and back too much. I am sure it would attract members.

Sections 17 & 18 (1947-48)
Section Representative:
Pauline Jackson (Garrett)

Jennifer Barton Jennifer tells us that she is 'keeping going' and she sends best wishes to all those in her year that are now reaching 90 years of age.

Johanna Merz Johanna cannot believe that she will be 90 in July this year! She is still living in the same house which was newly built in 1972. For company she has a dog, a Parson Russell, called Lukie. She has a large garden which she loves; not that she tends it herself as she has a gardener who comes when summoned.

Johanna has two children, Felicity who lives in the same terrace as her and Juliet who lives in Oxford. Both are in their 60s and Juliet (who is a cellist) rings twice a day. Felicity is a governor of a hospital nearby, which keeps her busy. Johanna's ex-husband Felix is now 92 and living in Wimbledon with his partner, who now has Parkinson's disease.

The only Westonbirt friend that she sees is **Susan Curtis-Bennett** who lives in Putney. Susan was well when she last saw her, and she received a cheerful Christmas card from her. Johanna misses her sister, **Penny Nairne,** who died in 2014. Johanna finishes by saying that she has three grandchildren - Alexander, Charlotte (who lives in Australia) and Rory, all of whom are doing really well, and she feels so lucky.

Section 16 (1946)
Section Representative:
Jane Reid

Acknowledgements of the 2019 Summer Newsletter and the 2020 AGM notice were received from **Patricia Krichauff (Faulkner)**

Elizabeth Watson (Allen) had a lovely 90th birthday party in 2019 and attended two 100th parties; both people sadly died at the beginning of the year. Elizabeth stayed a night with **Barbara Calwell (Lewis)** after one of the parties; it was nice to have catch-up time. She is also in contact with **Jean Speirs (Norman)**. She remembered staying behind at school as a sixth former to host Old Girls coming (some of whom took Elizabeth and another 'host' out to tea) for the fifteenth anniversary of the Association. When she emailed, she had hired a motorised wheelchair to take on holiday to the Algarve. In theory, 'It does 4 mph; heaven help the locals!'. In fact, it had difficulty in reaching a very slow walk; going out to the aeroplane, her escort begged (and was allowed) to push her. Otherwise, she was becoming less active due to back problems but had plenty of interests to keep her going.

Section 15 (1945)
Section Representative:
Serena Jones

Janet Briggs I attended Westonbirt School between 1942-1946. I have lived a varied life due to my connection with the Royal Navy, living in many parts of the world. I am keeping well, thanks to a lovely team of helpers and my family. I live in the house in which I was born, in Lacock, Wiltshire. I truly enjoy the garden and watching the birds and the passing of the seasons. I have five children, fifteen grandchildren and six great-grandchildren, all of which I see regularly, except for those who live in New Zealand, and they return when they're able. I'm still in contact with the odd "Old Girl", being one myself! I will be 93 next birthday, so have many memories and can still tell a tale or two!

June Fulford (Layborn) At 91, acquiring new ailments and attending funerals seem to be the order of the day! I did spend two weeks in a retirement home while daughter number 1 went on holiday (I don't live with her, but she could stop worrying about me), and enjoyed myself, very much to my surprise, as I was dreading it! Otherwise all as usual – two daughters, two sons-in-law, five grandchildren, four great-grandchildren - but no partridge! *(Yes, I get it... do you?! SJ)*

Mercia MacDermott (Adshead) I have realised with some excitement that I predate this school! At the time of writing, I am ninety-two, expecting to turn ninety-three in April 2020, and I feel very lucky that I am still able to live independently, doing my own shopping and cooking and able to walk quite long distances, including over the shingle of Worthing's beaches, looking for fossil sea-urchins and other interesting stones. Geology is one of my main interests. I am still president of the Friends of Worthing Museum.

One of my published books (*For Freedom and Perfection*, the biography of a Bulgarian Revolutionary, called Yane Sandansky), written some forty years ago, has been translated into French and will shortly be published in France by the Baudelaire Press.

Sections 13-14 (1943-44)
Section Representative:
Serena Jones

Editor's note: Mary Capey (Reynolds) *Mary wrote to Serena in the Autumn pointing out an error in the 2019 News: Mary's final paragraph erroneously appears under Jean Marr's news. So, Mary's news should have read: "I see **Elizabeth Wicks** and **Jenny Dean** from time to time. [.....] I have eight grandchildren and to date nine great-grandchildren, now very near and they all visit, or I visit them if collected." My apologies to both Mary and Jean for this error, as I suspect I added a separate entry in the wrong place...*

Gillian Blum (Gregory) 2019 was not a good year as I had a heart problem and had an operation in September. I am now well again and have just celebrated my 94th birthday, and also welcomed my fifth great grandchild into the family.

Rosemary Campbell (Fraser) A highlight this year was the wedding of one of my granddaughters, James' younger daughter Alice, to Simon Owtram in September. Otherwise, I have to say I am really feeling my age – I shall be 94 in October. Sadly, most of my contemporaries have died - like **Elizabeth Lambton (Fitzmaurice)** and **Elizabeth Burnett (Clark-Turner)** whose daughter is my goddaughter. I went to the former's funeral three or four years ago at Derry Hill Church, where I was confirmed on March 19th 1943. Miss Lilley, my housemistress, gave me a little book then which I still have called *The Profession of a Christian* by Peter Green. It's just right to show to my younger son, who is a clergyman in East Sussex. His church on Christmas Day last year was full to overflowing, standing room only – he speaks so well!

Mary Capey (Reynolds) Mary appears to be settled in her new flat with plenty of windows to view the mature trees and variety of birds in the garden. She still sings in the church choir and sees Elizabeth and Jenny quite regularly at their village hall lunches. I spoke to her in March (2020) and she was very grateful for my support to this section but asked if she could now become an inactive member and stop receiving mailings.

Jean Marr I was concerned that I had not heard from Jean this year as she has never before missed a year. I emailed the best researcher I know, **Jane Reid**, and she took up the difficult challenge of finding her. It turns out Jean has moved to a care home in Inverness, and Jane does have an address and phone number for her.

Sections 1-12 (1931-42)
Serena Jones (Sections 1-8)
Pauline Jackson (Section 9)
Rebecca Williams (Sections 10-12)

There are no active members in Sections 1 – 8, and no news from Sections 9 – 12.

Invitation to
Westonbirt Association Members

Westonbirt School always welcomes alumnae, whether on formal occasions such as Association Days, or for informal visits to reminisce about your school days. There's always something new to see, in terms of academic and extra-curricular activities, new buildings and projects to restore the old, and current pupils are always fascinated to meet their predecessors. You are also very welcome to bring your family, even if you have no daughters or granddaughters to follow in your academic footsteps!

In the interests of security, and to make sure we are able to welcome you on your preferred date, **please contact Mrs Rhiannon Roche, Head of Public Relations and Events, to arrange your visit by calling 01666 880333 or emailing rroche@westonbirt.gloucs.sch.uk.**

Whether or not you plan to visit the school in person, you may also like to visit our website, which is constantly being updated with school news and photos, as well as a picture gallery from the archives.

How to Contact the
Westonbirt Association

The Westonbirt Association database is kindly managed by the School, and so the School is now your first point of contact for any enquiries regarding the Association. **Mrs Rhiannon Roche, Head of Public Relations and Events**, will be able to direct you to the most appropriate person, according to the nature of your query. She will also be able to provide contact details for your Section Representative, whose personal information is no longer included in the News Magazine for the sake of their privacy.

Incidentally, please don't forget to let Rhiannon know **if your own contact details change**, so that we can keep you informed of Association matters and can find you if any of your former classmates are looking for you. If you use social media, you may also enjoy networking on the alumni Facebook page: *www.facebook.com/groups/108986984329/.*

Rhiannon works at the school full time, year-round, so is generally available during office hours. You may reach her via the main school telephone number, 01666 880333, or by emailing her at *rroche@westonbirt.gloucs.sch.uk*. She is always glad to hear from past pupils.

How to Order Copies
of the Westonbirt Association News

If you are a regular subscriber, you are welcome to go on receiving your printed copy, despatched by the News Finances and Distribution Officer, Jenny Webb, for as long as your account with her is in sufficient credit.

You may now also order the latest edition online, either in paperback or as an ebook, wherever you live in the world. Paperback copies will be printed in your local territory and sent at local postage rate. The ebook is available via all the mainstream ebook platforms, including Kindle, Kobo and iBooks, all around the world.

If you decide to move to online ordering while you still have credit in your Association News account, Jenny will refund the balance on request - or if you prefer, you may simply donate the balance to the Westonbirt Association Memorial Bursary Fund.

If you prefer not to order online or from Jenny, you should also be able to order a print copy from your local high street bookshop by providing them with the ISBN number of the latest edition. They should be able to get it in stock for you within a few days of your order.

We are confident that this is the best way forward for the long-term interests of the Association and the environment, and we hope it will also appeal to the younger generation (and many of the older ones!) who enjoy using digital technology. Please be assured, however, that we will always produce print copies for those who prefer them, and also for our substantial Association News archive.

Westonbirt Association
Memorial Bursary Fund

The Westonbirt Association Memorial Bursary was set up in the late 1940s in memory of the five former Westonbirt pupils who lost their lives during the Second World War while they were members of the Forces, Civil Defence or the Nursing Services.

The aim of the fund is to give a bursary each year to help fund the school fees of girls at the school. The Memorial Bursary is still running today, and each year the Association makes an award from this fund to help towards the sixth form fees of one or more pupils.

To be considered for the Memorial Bursary, girls must be nominated by the school in the spring of their Year 11. Candidates complete an application form and are interviewed by a panel from the Westonbirt Association Committee. The process provides good experience for later job and university applications, and, for the successful candidate, receipt of the award enhances their CV as well as providing welcome financial help. Once awarded, payment is made for both years of the recipient's sixth form.

Over the years, we have helped more than eighty pupils in this way. With income levels from investments so low at present, and school fees rising, new donations are always welcome to increase the value of the award.

How to Donate to the Memorial Bursary Fund

Cash donations

Payments may be made by cheque payable to "Westonbirt School" and should be clearly marked for the Westonbirt Association Memorial Bursary Fund.

Online by standing order

Please reference payment in the following format:

Account name: Westonbirt School
Sort code: 200384
Account number: 30951927
Bank: Barclays

Bequests

As the school is a charity, bequests are free from liability to inheritance tax. The following are suitable words to send to your solicitor with a request that the Westonbirt Association Memorial Bursary be included in your will:

"I bequeath to Westonbirt School in the county of Gloucestershire the sum of £x, free of duty, to be used for the purposes of the Westonbirt Association Memorial Bursary."

You might also wish to inform the school as follows:

"I intend to make a bequest to the school for the purposes of the Westonbirt Association Memorial Bursary."

GiftAid Declaration for the
Westonbirt Association Memorial Bursary

If you are a UK taxpayer, the school can reclaim tax on any gifts you make, via the Gift Aid scheme, provided you fill in the declaration form below in full and return it with your first gift.

Please treat as Gift Aid donations all qualifying gifts of money made *(please circle as applicable)*: today / in the past 4 years / in the future

I enclose a donation of £.......... as a contribution to the Westonbirt Association Memorial Bursary.

I confirm I have paid or will pay an amount of income tax or capital gains tax for each tax year (6 April to 5 April) that is at least equal to the amount of tax that Westonbirt School and all other charities that I donate to will reclaim on my gifts for that tax year. I understand that other taxes such as VAT and council tax do not qualify. I understand the charity will reclaim 25p on every £1 that I give on or after 6 April 2008.

Title_____ Forename _____

Surname_____

Address_____

Postcode_____

Signature_____

Date_____

Please notify Westonbirt School if you want to cancel this declaration OR change your name or home address OR no longer pay sufficient tax on your income and/or capital gains. If you pay income tax at the higher or additional tax rate and want to receive the additional tax relief due to you, you must include all your Gift Aid donations on your self-assessment tax return.

Please send donations and the completed form to:
The Finance Manager, The Bursary, Westonbirt School
Tetbury, Gloucestershire GL8 8QG
Registered Charity Number 311715

www.ingramcontent.com/pod-product-compliance
Lightning Source LLC
Chambersburg PA
CBHW070936030426
42336CB00014BA/2704